Study Guide for the
Business Education Test

▶ ▶ ▶ ▶ ▶ ▶ ▶ ▶ ▶ ▶ ▶ ▶

A PUBLICATION OF EDUCATIONAL TESTING SERVICE

Table of Contents
Study Guide for the *Business Education* Test

▶   ▶   ▶   ▶   ▶   ▶   ▶   ▶   ▶   ▶   ▶   ▶

TABLE OF CONTENTS

Chapter 1

Introduction to the *Business Education* Test and Suggestions for Using This Study Guide

▶ ▶ ▶ ▶ ▶ ▶ ▶ ▶ ▶ ▶ ▶ ▶

Introduction to *Business Education*

The *Business Education* test (0100) is designed for prospective secondary business education teachers. The test is designed to reflect current standards for knowledge, skills, and abilities in business education. Educational Testing Service (ETS) works in collaboration with the National Council for Accreditation of Teacher Education (NCATE), along with teacher educators, higher education content specialists, and accomplished practicing teachers in the field of business education to keep the test updated and representative of current standards.

The *Business Education* test consists of 120 multiple-choice questions and covers seven major areas, in the following proportions:

Content Category	Approximate Number of Questions	Approximate Percentage of Examination
• United States Economic Systems	12	10%
• Money Management	17	14%
• Business and Its Environment	13	11%
• Professional Business Education	24	20%
• Processing Information	20	17%
• Office Procedures and Management, Communications, and Employability Skills	17	14%
• Accounting and Marketing	17	14%

Test takers have two hours to complete the test.

The test is not intended to assess teaching skills but rather to demonstrate the candidate's fundamental knowledge in the major areas of business education. Calculators are allowed if they do not have a QWERTY keyboard.

Suggestions for using the "Study Topics" chapter of this study guide

The *Business Education* test is different from a final exam or other tests you may have taken in that it is comprehensive — that is, it covers material you may have learned in several courses during more than one year. It requires you to synthesize information you have learned from many sources and to understand the subject as a whole.

This test is also very different from the SAT® or other assessments of your reading, writing, and mathematical skills. You may have heard it said that you can't study for the SAT — that is, you should have learned these skills throughout your school years, and you can't learn reading or reasoning skills shortly before you take the exam. You can *practice* taking the SAT and skills tests like it to become more adept at applying the skills to the particular format of the test. The *Business Education* test, on the other hand, assesses a domain you *can* review for and *can* prepare to be tested on. Therefore, you should review for and prepare for your test, not merely practice with the question formats. A thorough review of the material covered on the test will significantly increase your likelihood of success. Moreover, studying for your licensing exam is a great opportunity to reflect on your field and develop a deeper understanding of it before you begin to teach the subject matter to others. As you prepare to take the test, you may find it particularly helpful to think about how you would apply the study topics and sample exercises to your own clinical experience that you obtained in schools during your teacher preparation program. Your student teaching experience will be especially relevant to your thinking about the materials in the study guide.

We recommend the following approach for using the "Study Topics" chapters to prepare for the test.

Become familiar with the test content. Learn what will be assessed in the test, covered in chapter 3.

Assess how well you know the content in each area. It is quite likely that you will need to study in most or all of the areas. After you learn what the test contains, you should assess your knowledge in each area. How well do you know the material? In which areas do you need to learn more before you take the test?

Develop a study plan. Assess what you need to study and create a realistic plan for studying. You can develop your study plan in any way that works best for you. A "Study Plan" form is included in Appendix A at the end of the book as a possible way to structure your planning. Remember that this is a licensure test and covers a great deal of material. Plan to review carefully. You will need to allow time to find the books and other materials, time to read the material and take notes, and time to go over your notes.

Identify study materials. Most of the material covered by the test is contained in standard introductory textbooks. If you do not own introductory texts that cover all the areas, you may want to borrow one or more from friends or from a library. You may also want to obtain a copy of your state's standards for business education. (One way to find these standards quickly is to go to the Web site for your state's Department of Education.) The textbooks used in secondary classrooms may also prove useful to you, since they also present the material you need to know. Use standard school and college introductory textbooks and other reliable, professionally prepared materials. Don't rely heavily on information provided by friends or from searching the World Wide Web. Neither of these sources is as uniformly reliable as textbooks.

Work through your study plan. You may want to work alone, or you may find it more helpful to work with a group or with a mentor. Work through the topics and questions provided in chapter 3. Be able to define and discuss the topics in your own words rather than memorizing definitions from books. If you are working with a group or mentor, you can also try informal quizzes and questioning techniques.

Proceed to the practice questions. Once you have completed your review, you are ready to benefit from the "Practice Questions" portion of this guide.

Suggestions for using the "Practice Questions" and "Right Answers and Explanations for the Practice Questions" chapters

Read chapter 4 ("Don't Be Defeated by Multiple-choice Questions"). This chapter will sharpen your skills in reading and answering questions. Succeeding on multiple-choice questions requires careful focus on the question, an eye for detail, and patient sifting of the answer choices.

Answer the practice questions in chapter 5. Make your own test-taking conditions as similar to actual testing conditions as you can. Work on the practice questions in a quiet place without distractions. Remember that the practice questions are only examples of the way the topics are covered in the test. The test will have different questions.

Score the practice questions. Go through the detailed answers in chapter 6 ("Right Answers and Explanations") and mark the questions you answered correctly and the ones you missed. Look over the explanations of the questions you missed and see if you understand them.

Decide whether you need more review. After you have looked at your results, decide if there are areas that you need to brush up on before taking the actual test. (The practice questions are grouped by topic, which may help you to spot areas of particular strength or weakness.) Go back to your textbooks and reference materials to see if the topics are covered there. You might also want to go over your questions with a friend or teacher who is familiar with the subjects.

Assess your readiness. Do you feel confident about your level of understanding in each of the areas? If not, where do you need more work? If you feel ready, complete the checklist in chapter 7 ("Are You Ready?") to double-check that you've thought through the details. If you need more information about registration or the testing situation itself, use the resources in Appendix B: "For More Information."

Chapter 2
Background Information on the Praxis Series™ Assessments

▶   ▶   ▶   ▶   ▶   ▶   ▶   ▶   ▶   ▶   ▶   ▶

What are the Praxis Series Subject Assessments?

The Praxis Series Subject Assessments are designed by Educational Testing Service (ETS) to assess your knowledge of the subject area you plan to teach, and they are a part of the licensing procedure in many states. This study guide covers an assessment that tests your knowledge of the actual content you hope to be licensed to teach. Your state has adopted The Praxis Series tests because it wants to be certain that you have achieved a specified level of mastery of your subject area before it grants you a license to teach in a classroom.

The Praxis Series tests are part of a national testing program, meaning that the test covered in this study guide is used in more than one state. The advantage of taking Praxis tests is that if you want to move to another state that uses The Praxis Series tests, you can transfer your scores to that state. Passing scores are set by states, however, so if you are planning to apply for licensure in another state, you may find that passing scores are different. You can find passing scores for all states that use The Praxis Series tests in the *Understanding Your Praxis Scores* pamphlet, available either in your college's School of Education or by calling (609) 771-7395.

What is licensure?

Licensure in any area—medicine, law, architecture, accounting, cosmetology—is an assurance to the public that the person holding the license has demonstrated a certain level of competence. The phrase used in licensure is that the person holding the license *will do no harm*. In the case of teacher licensing, a license tells the public that the person holding the license can be trusted to educate children competently and professionally.

Because a license makes such a serious claim about its holder, licensure tests are usually quite demanding. In some fields licensure tests have more than one part and last for more than one day. Candidates for licensure in all fields plan intensive study as part of their professional preparation: some join study groups, others study alone. But preparing to take a licensure test is, in all cases, a professional activity. Because it assesses your entire body of knowledge or skill for the field you want to enter, preparing for a licensure exam takes planning, discipline, and sustained effort. Studying thoroughly is highly recommended.

Why does my state require The Praxis Series Assessments?

Your state chose The Praxis Series Assessments because the tests assess the breadth and depth of content— called the "domain" of the test—that your state wants its teachers to possess before they begin to teach. The level of content knowledge, reflected in the passing score, is based on recommendations of panels of teachers and teacher educators in each subject area in each state. The state licensing agency and, in some states, the state legislature ratify the passing scores that have been recommended by panels of teachers. You can find out the passing score required for The Praxis Series Assessments in your state by looking in the pamphlet *Understanding Your Praxis Scores*, which is free from ETS (see previous page). If you look through this pamphlet, you will see that not all states use the same test modules, and even when they do, the passing scores can differ from state to state.

What kinds of tests are The Praxis Series Subject Assessments?

Two kinds of tests comprise The Praxis Series Subject Assessments: multiple choice (for which you select your answer from a list of choices) and constructed response (for which you write a response of your own). Multiple-choice tests can survey a wider domain because they can ask more questions in a limited period of time. Constructed-response tests have far fewer questions, but the questions require you to demonstrate the depth of your knowledge in the area covered.

What do the tests measure?

The Praxis Series Subject Assessments are tests of content knowledge. They measure your understanding of the subject area you want to teach. The multiple-choice tests measure a broad range of knowledge across your content area. The constructed-response tests measure your ability to explain in depth a few essential topics in your subject area. The content-specific pedagogy tests, most of which are constructed-response, measure your understanding of how to teach certain fundamental concepts in your field. The tests do not measure your actual teaching ability, however. They measure your knowledge of your subject and of how to teach it. The teachers in your field who help us design and write these tests, and the states that require these tests, do so in the belief that knowledge of subject area is the first requirement for licensing. Your teaching ability is a skill that is measured in other ways: observation, videotaped teaching, or portfolios are typically used by states to measure teaching ability. Teaching combines many complex skills, only some of which can be measured by a single test. The Praxis Series Subject Assessments are designed to measure how thoroughly you understand the material in the subject areas in which you want to be licensed to teach.

How were these tests developed?

ETS began the development of The Praxis Series Subject Assessments with a survey. For each subject, teachers around the country in various teaching situations were asked to judge which knowledge and skills a beginning teacher in that subject needs to possess. Professors in schools of education who prepare teachers were asked the same questions. These responses were ranked in order of importance and sent out to hundreds of teachers for review. All of the responses to these surveys (called "job analysis surveys") were analyzed to summarize the judgments of these professionals. From their consensus, we developed the specifications for the multiple-choice and constructed-response tests. Each subject area had a committee of practicing teachers and teacher educators who wrote these specifications (guidelines). The specifications were reviewed and eventually approved by teachers. From the test specifications, groups of teachers and professional test developers created test questions.

When your state adopted The Praxis Series Subject Assessments, local panels of practicing teachers and teacher educators in each subject area met to examine the tests question by question and evaluate each question for its relevance to beginning teachers in your state. This is called a "validity study." A test is considered "valid" for a job if it measures what people must know and be able to do on that job. For the test to be adopted in your state, teachers in your state must judge that it is valid.

These teachers and teacher educators also performed a "standard-setting study"; that is, they went through the tests question by question and decided, through a rigorous process, how many questions a beginning teacher should be able to answer correctly. From this study emerged a recommended passing score. The final passing score was approved by your state's Department of Education.

In other words, throughout the development process, practitioners in the teaching field—teachers and teacher educators—have determined what the tests would contain. The practitioners in your state determined which tests would be used for licensure in your subject area and helped decide what score would be needed to achieve licensure. This is how professional licensure works in most fields: those who are already licensed oversee the licensing of new practitioners. When you pass The Praxis Series Subject Assessments, you and the practitioners in your state can be assured that you have the knowledge required to begin practicing your profession.

Chapter 3
Study Topics for the *Business Education* Test

Introduction to the test

The *Business Education* test is designed to measure the subject-area knowledge and competencies necessary for a beginning teacher of business education in a secondary school. The topics for questions are typically those covered in introductory courses in a college-level business education curriculum, although some questions of a more advanced nature are included, because secondary-school instructors must understand the subject matter from a more advanced viewpoint than that presented to their students. Also, since a major goal of business education is to have students develop an understanding of accounting, marketing, and the environment of business, these areas are included in the assessment. The questions include definition of terms, comprehension of critical concepts, application, analysis, and problem solving.

This chapter is intended to help you organize your preparation for the test and to give you a clear indication about the depth and breadth of the knowledge required for success on the test.

Using the topic lists that follow: You are not expected to be an expert on all aspects of the topics that follow. You should understand the major characteristics of each topic, recognize the minor topics, and have some familiarity with the subtopics. Virtually all accredited undergraduate business education programs address the majority of these topics, subtopics, and even minor topics.

You are likely to find that the topics below are covered by most introductory business education textbooks and textbooks for related fields (such as economics, marketing, and accounting), but a general survey textbook may not cover all of the subtopics. Consult materials and resources, including lecture and laboratory notes, from all your business education coursework. You should be able to match up specific topics and subtopics with what you have covered in your courses in education, economics, accounting, office procedures, and so on.

Try not to be overwhelmed by the volume and scope of content knowledge in this guide. An overview such as this that lists business education topics does not offer you a great deal of context. Although a specific term may not seem familiar as you see it here, you might find you could understand it when it is applied to a real-life situation. Many of the items on the actual Praxis test will provide you with a context within which to apply to these topics or terms, as you will see when you look at the practice questions in Chapter 5.

Special questions marked with stars: Interspersed throughout the list of topics are questions that are outlined in boxes and preceded by stars (★). These questions are intended to help you test your knowledge of fundamental concepts and your ability to apply fundamental concepts to situations in the classroom or the real world. Most of the questions require you to combine several pieces of knowledge in order to formulate an integrated understanding and response. If you spend time on these questions, you will gain increased understanding and facility with the subject matter covered on the test. You might want to discuss these questions and your answers with a teacher or mentor.

Note that the questions marked with stars are not short-answer or multiple-choice and that this study guide does not provide the answers. The questions marked with stars are intended as study questions, not practice questions. Thinking about

[Handwritten left margin, rotated: Banks & credit unions hold reserves in vault or at TMS, The FR controls the reserves by lending $ & changes the rate]

the answers to them should improve your understanding of fundamental concepts and will probably help you answer a broad range of questions on the test. For example, the following box with a star appears in the list of study topics under "Government and Banking":

★ How does the Federal Reserve control the flow of money in the United States?

[Handwritten: the supply is dollar bills/coins + is measured by sum of currency, ck acct, savings]

If you think about this question, perhaps jotting down some notes on the factors involved in monetary policy, you will review your knowledge of how the Federal Reserve System works, and you will have probably prepared yourself to answer multiple-choice questions similar to the one below:

Which of the following actions by the Federal Reserve System would be most likely to increase consumer spending?

(A) Increasing reserve requirements for member banks

(B) Increasing the discount rate to member banks

(C) Decreasing the discount rate to member banks

(D) Selling large amounts of government securities

(E) Keeping reserve requirements of member banks constant

(The correct answer is (C). A reduction in the discount rate — the rate charged commercial banks to borrow money from the Federal Reserve — encourages banks to lend money, promoting consumer spending.)

[Handwritten bottom left:]
+ Sole - easily formed, ∠ gov regul., ∅ corp. income tx
− Sole - hard to get lg $, personal liab., life limit of busn
+ partner - ↓ cost & easily formed
− partner unlimited liab, limit to life of org, difficult to transfer ownership, difficult to raise ↑ capital

United States Economic Systems

◆ Free Enterprise System
  • What it is *[Handwritten: Freedom of a private busn to operate competitively for a Pwl min gov reservation]*
  • How it functions *[Handwritten: when ownership, capital & entre. are comb to create econ activity]*

★ What is free enterprise?

★ How does free enterprise function in a capitalistic society? *[Handwritten: Thru the busn aspect of supply & demand from flow of good & serv]*

  • Impact of entrepreneurship on the free enterprise system *[Handwritten: give the owner the right to make own choices purchase, sell, labor - busn structure]*
  • How businesses are organized and managed *[Handwritten: sole 80%, partnership, corporation]*

★ Why is it important to delegate duties and responsibilities?

★ What are the ways in which businesses can establish lines of authority?

★ How does a budget help give a business stability?

★ What are the types of management styles?

  • Forms of business organization *[Handwritten: indiv, partnership, corporation]*

★ What is a sole proprietorship? *[Handwritten: owned + managed by 1 person]*
★ What are the advantages of a corporation over a partnership? *[Handwritten: capital]*

  • Basic principles of business management *[Handwritten: P, L, O, C]*
  • Importance of preparing and using a business plan *[Handwritten: ✓ plan for ur busn + can be shown to potential investors]*

◆ Government and Banking
  • How fiscal and monetary policies impact the economy *[Handwritten: expenditures & taxation. Attempts to control economy by controlling int. rates & $ supply.]*
[Handwritten: corporation is an legal entity separate from owner]

[Handwritten bottom:]
+ corp - unlimited life, ease of transfer ownership, limited liability
− corp - earning maybe 2x taxed, set up is expensive + time consuming

★ How does the Federal Reserve control the flow of money in the United States?

★ Who controls the Federal Reserve? *under the US gov. by Congress, funding comes from US Trees*

★ What is the national debt, and how is it calculated? *outstand. gov. debt money taken in − $ spent*

- Gross domestic product (GDP) *Amt of goods service produced in 1 yr*
- Personal and business taxation

★ How do itemized deductions affect a personal income tax return?

★ What taxes paid by employees are also paid by businesses? *SS + medicare*

- Banking regulations
▶ Economic Principles
- Inflation and deflation

↑ in Price ↓ $ value → ↓ in P, ↑ value

★ What are the characteristics of an inflationary period?

★ During a recession, what effect does increased government spending have on the economy? *It doesn't effect econ growth*

- Supply-and-demand theory

★ What is the point at which the supply-and-demand curves intersect? *Equilibrium*

★ How does increasing supply and decreasing demand affect prices?

- Price systems

★ What is the law of diminishing returns? *Eagle Band − No more space to add mach, extra hours, more employees*

- International trade *not enough sup., mach Breaks Labor input gets ↓*

(left margin handwritten notes)
D↑ S is the same = ↑ P ↓ Q
D↓ S is the same = ↓ P ↑ Q
S↑ D is the same = ↓ P ↑ Q
S↓ D is the same = ↑ P ↓ Q

★ What impact would decreasing exports have on the economy?

- Labor-management relations

Money Management

▶ Business Mathematics
- Calculation of unit price

★ If a box of cereal is $4.99 for 24 oz., what is the cost per oz.? *.207*

- Price increase or decrease calculations

★ If a can of paint increased in price from $24.00 to $30.00, what is the percent of the price increase? *30 − 24 = 6 ÷ 24 = 25%*

- Calculation of commission on gross sales

★ Use the chart below to calculate commission on gross sales of $57,000.

Sales	Percent of Commission
$10,000 – $20,000	5%
$21,000 – $30,000	6%
$31,000 – $40,000	7%
$41,000 – $50,000	8%
$51,000 – $60,000	9%

- Calculation of simple interest

★ What would be the interest charged on $6,500 at 7% for 6 months?

(Using the formula interest = principal x rate x time, the calculation would be $6,500 x 7% x 6/12, or $227.50.)

- Payroll calculations

★ Calculate the net pay for the following employee:

Hours	Rate	FICA	State Tax	Insurance	Net Pay
36.5	$12.44/hr.	6%	7.8%	2.2%	

454.06   27.24   35.42   999   381.4

- Consumer education
  - budgeting

★ If a family's budget included the following— monthly rent, insurance premiums, entertainment, and car payment—which cost would be variable?

  - consumer rights and responsibilities
  - marketplace decisions

- Personal finance
  - banking
  - investing
  - credit
  - present-value theory-- *Current worth of future*
  - risk management – *ID, Assessment, prioritization of risk*

I = P x R x T

★ Be able to calculate the maturity date of a 90-day loan.

★ Be able to calculate monthly interest on a credit card statement, given the balance and the annual percentage rate.

Business and Its Environment

- Job Standards for Various Career Clusters
- Work Standards for Employees
- Business Ethics and Policies

★ Is it acceptable for an employee to take a company laptop computer home for personal use?

- How Employees Work with Each Other
- Employee Evaluations and Their Importance to the Management Plan
- Ways to Measure Productivity in the Workplace
- Business Contracts and How They are Prepared

★ What is the Statute of Frauds? *requires contract in writing to prevent fraud*

★ How does duress affect the validity of a contract? *coercion to perform an act normally not performed*

- Principal and Agent – *arrangement between the agent on behalf of the principal + is guided by a contract*

★ What are the duties and liabilities of the principal and agent?

- Types of Insurance *Health, Life, Auto*
- Laws that Pertain to Consigned Goods – *goods shipped to a customer, not pd for*
- Types of Negotiable Instruments *Draft, promissory Note, Cert. of Deposit*

★ What are the characteristics of a negotiable instrument?

★ What are the types of endorsements that can be used on a check? *Blank, special, qualified restrictive, Deposit only*

- Types of Torts and Tort Law – *Intentional, negligence*
- Bankruptcy Laws – *Liquidating assets to pay their debt or creating a repmt*

★ What are the different types of bankruptcy available under the Bankruptcy Act of 1938? *9, 12, 13, 15*

- Forms of Consumer Legislation
any law that protects an indiv. against busn
lemon, safety, banking, unfair trade
competition, product liab., Licensing, Discrimination theft

◗ Discrimination Laws

◗ Labor laws and Laws Pertaining to Negotiations

◗ Laws in the Global Economy

Professional Business Education

◗ Professionalism

- Familiarity with professional organizations and literature associated with Business Education

- Ethical behavior in the classroom and/or workplace

- Working with colleagues and supervisors

- Ways to promote a school's Business Education program
  - community advisory council
  - newsletters
  - school publications

◗ Current Trends and Issues

- Types of equipment currently used in classrooms

- Use of simulations in the classroom

- Use and interpretation of current research in Business Education

◗ Methodology/Teaching Strategies

- Competency-based instruction *focuses on outcomes of learning, based on the changing needs of students/teachers*

- Creating reliable and valid assessments

- Cooperative Education Work-Experience Programs

- Instructional strategies for special needs students *accomodation, modification, oral instruction, immediate feedback, activities short*

- *provide concrete touch, hear, smell need lots of praise encourage, group activity* Components of a complete teaching objective *state dictates curriculm*

- Matching software to curricular objectives

- Teaching to the affective and cognitive domains

◗ Student Organizations

- Future Business Leaders of America (FBLA)

- Phi Beta Lambda (PBL)

- DECA—A Marketing Association for Students (DECA)

★ What are the goals and objectives of each organization?

★ Which organizations serve high schools? colleges?

◗ Federal Vocational Legislation

★ What is the objective of the Carl D. Perkins Act of 1963 and reauthorization of 1998?

◗ Mission/Objectives of Business Education

- Lifelong learning

- Occupational preparation

- Responsibilities to the business community

- Economic literacy

- Training and retraining

- Preparation for postsecondary education

◗ Community Relations

- Role of the school's advisory council

- Input provided by advisory council that is critical to the curriculum in Business Education

★ How can individuals from an advisory council be utilized for instruction within the classroom?

★ What kind of alliances may be formed between the business community and the school that will enhance education?

◆ Curriculum Planning and Program Development
  • Developing programs for Business Education classrooms
    ▪ needs assessments
    ▪ parts of an objective
    ▪ Bloom's taxonomy of higher-order thinking skills

★ What is the difference between teaching to the cognitive domain *vs.* the affective domain?

  • Alternative methods of assessment (testing) relating to skill and general business classes

★ What methods of assessment are best suited for skills classes?

  • Teaching strategies for special needs students

◆ Department Management
  • Role of a department supervisor
  • Departmental needs and priorities
    ▪ equipment
    ▪ supplies
    ▪ staffing
  • Departmental budget preparation

◆ Classroom Management
  • Daily attendance records

★ Why must daily attendance records be obtained for each student in the class?

  • Safety hazards present with equipment being used in the classroom

★ How do OSHA rules and regulations pertain to a classroom setting? *parents send children to school + expect safe environment. Schools fall + are protected by OSHA ~ must meet the safety requirements*

  • Lesson plans
    ▪ development
    ▪ utilization
    ▪ revision
  • Counseling in Business Education
  • Career awareness
    ▪ guest speakers
  • Career exploration
    ▪ job shadowing
    ▪ cooperative work-experience programs
  • Career preparation
    ▪ resume preparation
    ▪ letter of application
    ▪ interview techniques
  • Employment trends

Processing Information

◆ Keyboarding
  • Familiarity with the keys on a computer keyboard and their functions

★ What is a macro?

- Copy styles
  - unarranged
  - formatted
- Production keying and its use in a classroom

▶ Production
- Mailable documents

★ What tasks are necessary, in what order, to prepare and disseminate a completed document?

- Types of software packages and their uses

★ To generate a chart or graph from a numeric table, which type of software package would be utilized?

★ What are electronic ways of communicating a document from one site to another?

▶ Word Processing
- Important commands and their capabilities
  - search/replace
  - spell check
  - mail merge
- Formatting functions in a word processing program.

★ What are margins, tabs, bullets, and how are they set?

▶ Proofreading and Editing
- Proofreading symbols used in editing copy

★ Which proofreading symbol would be used to indicate that something should be double spaced?

▶ Database and Spreadsheet Applications
- Capabilities and major features of these types of software
- Student "work simulation packets"
- Matching a specific task to a specific kind of software

▶ Graphics

★ What are the steps in downloading a graphic from the Internet?

★ How are graphics sized (made smaller or larger) within a document?

▶ Computer Literacy
- Input/output devices used with personal computers
- Acronyms and various computer terms

★ What is the difference between RAM and ROM? *random access mem* *read only mem* internal comp. memory — cannot be written to

★ What are the three elements of data processing? input, processing, storage output

★ What is a LAN? local Area network

- Default settings
  - what they are
  - how to change them
  - settings for a given application

★ What are the advantages of using electronic mail?

★ How is an attachment added to an e-mail message?

★ What are the advantages and disadvantages of using magnetic media in processing and saving data?

▶ Internet Technology

• Parts of an Internet address (e.g., http://www.ets.org)

• Internet terminology

★ What is spamming? *junk mail*

★ What are cookies? *tracks places, interest, patterns*

Office Procedures, and Management, Communications, and Employability Skills

▶ Office Procedures and Management

• Managerial roles

▪ office manager

▪ treasurer

▪ comptroller

▪ business administrator

▪ chief executive officer

▪ chief financial officer

• Support staff roles

▪ receptionists

▪ secretaries

▪ records management staff

▪ other support personnel

• Records management procedures

★ What are the types of media used to store office records?

★ What are the kinds of files that are used in managing paper records?

• Handling of mail in an office

★ What are the kinds and classes of mail? *Express, Priority, 1st Class, stand, period, Pkg*

★ What are the two-letter postal abbreviations requested by the U.S. Postal Service for use on envelopes? *State*

• Flow of work in a business operation

★ In what ways can the flow of work be improved?

• Arranging travel and meetings

★ How is an itinerary created, and how is it used?

★ What customs are appropriate in foreign countries?

★ What is an agenda, and why is it necessary?

▶ Business Communications

• Proper techniques for public speaking

★ What are the steps used to develop an effective presentation?

• Speaking aids

▪ equipment

▪ computer programs

★ What types of media can be used when preparing and giving a presentation?

★ How do computerized presentation program packages enhance a presentation?

- Business letters
  - types
  - correct formats

★ What are the parts of a business letter?

- Proper telephone techniques

★ What are the time zones throughout the U.S. and the world?

★ How should a difficult phone caller be handled?

- Types of equipment used in an office and their function

★ What are the different types of computer networks?

★ What is the difference between a local area network and a wide area network?

- Barriers to communication

★ What are some nonverbal forms of communication that create barriers for the sender of the information?

▶ Employability Skills
  - Developing a resume

★ What are the parts of a basic resume?

- Letters of application
- Procedures used during a job interview

★ What are some questions that you should ask at a job interview?

★ What information should *not* be discussed at an interview?

- Laws relating to sexual harassment
- Forms of bias related to hiring and terminating employees
- Sources of information to locate jobs
- Termination from a job

★ What are the reasons that an employer might terminate an employee?

★ Under what circumstances can an employee receive unemployment compensation?

Accounting

▶ Account Classification (Asset, Liability, Owner's Equity, Income, Cost, Expense)

▶ Debit and Credit Theory

▶ Sides of Each Account Classification
  - Increase
  - Decrease

★ If a cash payment is made for electricity, how will the payment affect the Net Income on the Income Statement?

★ How does an increased amount of sales returns affect the Owner's Equity on the Balance Sheet?

▶ Basic Accounting Cycle
  - Steps
  - Sequence

★ What role do source documents have in the initial steps of account analysis?

★ How does each step of the accounting cycle impact the next?

◗ Components of a Journal Entry that Uses Double-Entry Accounting Methods

◗ Posting to Various Types of Ledger Accounts
- The need
- The process

◗ Calculating the Depreciation of Equipment and Other Assets

★ Straight line

★ Sum-of-the-year's digits

★ Declining balance

◗ Calculating the Cost of Merchandise Sold

★ Given the amounts for the Beginning Inventory, Sales, Purchases, and Ending Inventory, calculate the cost of merchandise sold.

◗ End-of-fiscal-period Statements of Account
- Preparation
- Calculations required to prepare them
- Analysis
- Components of statements
  - trial balance
  - worksheet
  - income statement
  - balance sheet
  - post-closing trial balance

★ How do closing entries impact the accounts affected?

★ Why are closing entries needed when preparing an end-of-fiscal-period statement?

◗ Use of Computers and Computer Software

Marketing

◗ Components of the Marketing Mix

◗ Legislation Affecting Marketing and Sales of Products
- Copyright
- Trademark
- Patent

◗ Types of Sales Techniques
- Telephone marketing
- Personal selling
- Pre-approach

★ What circumstances favor one kind of sales technique over another?

◗ Types of Advertising Used by Business Owners and Managers
- Television
- Radio
- Print
- Direct mail
- Outdoor
- Internet

★ What are the benefits and relative costs of each type of advertising?

◗ Methods of Displaying Merchandise Within
a Store's Layout

- Seasonal goods

- Staple goods

- Luxury goods

- Convenience goods

◗ Inventory Control and Management
Techniques

- Types of inventory-control systems

- Physical inventory *vs.* perpetual inventory — paper

- Management of stock (floor stock and
back stock)

- Shoplifting and employee pilfering

◗ Inventory Pricing Methods

- Average cost

- LIFO (last-in first-out)

- FIFO (first-in first-out)

★ When is it appropriate to use one method
rather than another? cellphone minutes

Chapter 4
Don't Be Defeated by Multiple-choice Questions

▶ ▶ ▶ ▶ ▶ ▶ ▶ ▶ ▶ ▶ ▶ ▶

Why multiple-choice tests take time

When you take the practice questions, you will see that there are very few simple identification questions such as "Which of the following is an accurate definition of a byte?" When The Praxis Series™ Assessments were first being developed by teachers and teacher educators across the country, it was almost universally agreed that prospective teachers should be able to analyze situations, synthesize material, and apply knowledge to specific examples. In short, they should be able to think as well as to recall specific facts, figures, or formulas. Consequently, you will find that you are being asked to think and to solve problems on your test. Such activity takes more time than simply answering identification questions.

In addition, questions that require you to analyze situations, synthesize material, and apply knowledge are usually longer than are simple identification questions. The Praxis Series test questions often present you with something to read (a case study, a sample of student work, a chart or graph) and ask you questions based on your reading. Strong reading skills are required, and you must read carefully. Both on this test and as a teacher, you will need to process and use what you read efficiently.

If you know your reading skills are not strong, you may want to take a reading course. College campuses have reading labs that can help you strengthen your reading skills.

Understanding multiple-choice questions

You will probably notice that the word order (or syntax) in multiple-choice questions is different from the word order you're used to seeing in ordinary things you read, like newspapers or textbooks. One of the reasons for this difference is that many such questions contain the phrase "which of the following."

The purpose of the phrase "which of the following" is to limit your choice of answers only to the list given. For example, look at this question.

Which of the following is a flavor made from beans?

(A) Strawberry

(B) Cherry

(C) Vanilla

(D) Mint

You may know that chocolate and coffee are flavors made from beans also. But they are not listed, and the question asks you to select from among the list that follows ("which of the following"). So the answer has to be the only bean-derived flavor in the list: vanilla.

Notice that the answer can be substituted for the phrase "which of the following." In the question above, you could insert "vanilla" for "which of the following" and have the sentence "Vanilla is a flavor made from beans." Sometimes it helps to cross out "which of the following" and insert the various choices. You may want to give this technique a try as you answer various multiple-choice questions in the practice test.

Also, looking carefully at the "which of the following" phrase helps you to focus on what the question is asking you to find and on the answer choices. In the simple example above, all of the answer choices are flavors. Your job is to decide which of the flavors is the one made from beans.

The vanilla bean question is pretty straightforward. But the phrase "which of the following" can also be found in more challenging questions. Look at this question:

> In the evaluation of advanced keyboarding skill, which of the following should be given the most weight?
>
> (A) Techniques of keyboarding
>
> (B) Basic skill competencies
>
> (C) Production skill competencies
>
> (D) Work attitudes and habits
>
> (E) Straight-copy skill

The placement of "which of the following" tells you that the list of choices is a list of criteria for evaluating advanced keyboarding skill. What are you supposed to find as an answer? You are supposed to find the choice that should be given the most weight when you are making such an evaluation of a student.

Sometimes it helps to put the question in your own words. Here, you could paraphrase the question as "If I were evaluating a student for advanced keyboarding skill, what would I consider most important?" Since keyboarding skill at the advanced level is most concerned with overall production skill competencies, the correct answer is (C).

You may find that it helps to circle or underline each of the critical details of the question in your test book so that you don't miss any of them. It's only by looking at all parts of the question carefully that you will have all of the information you need to answer the question.

Circle or underline the critical parts of what is being asked in this question.

> Which of the following describes the effect of federal vocational legislation on business education in the United States?
>
> (A) It has had little impact in that business education is not covered by such legislation.
>
> (B) It has served to standardize high school business education offerings nationwide.
>
> (C) It has placed business education youth organizations, such as FBLA and DECA, under central federal authority.
>
> (D) It has provided states with financial assistance for the operation of vocational business education programs.
>
> (E) It has provided numerous textbooks and other instructional materials published by the United States Government Printing Office.

Here is one possible way you may have annotated the question:

> Which of the following describes the <u>effect</u> of <u>federal vocational legislation</u> on <u>business education</u> in the United States?
>
> (A) It has had little impact in that business education is not covered by such legislation.
>
> (B) It has served to standardize high school business education offerings nationwide.
>
> (C) It has placed business education youth organizations, such as FBLA and DECA, under central federal authority.
>
> (D) It has provided states with financial assistance for the operation of vocational business education programs.
>
> (E) It has provided numerous textbooks and other instructional materials published by the United States Government Printing Office.

After spending a few moments with the question, you can probably see that you are being asked to recognize how federal vocational legislation has affected business education. Most of the answer choices — (B), (C), and (E) — suggest that this legislation has greater scope than it actually has. (A) suggests that it has almost no effect. In fact, it has provided mostly funding. The correct answer, therefore, is (D).

The important thing is understanding what the question is asking. With enough practice, you should be able to determine what any question is asking. Knowing the answer is, of course, a different matter, but you have to understand a question before you can answer it.

Understanding questions containing "NOT," "LEAST," "EXCEPT"

In addition to "which of the following" and details that must be understood, the words "NOT," "EXCEPT," and "LEAST" often make comprehension of test questions more difficult. Because they are easily (and frequently) overlooked, these words are always capitalized when they directly impact the task presented by a test question.

For the following test question, determine what kind of answer you're looking for and what the details of the question are.

> A six-step procedure is usually associated with the preparation of correspondence for filing. Which of the following is NOT considered a part of the procedure?
>
> (A) Inspecting and indexing
>
> (B) Date stamping
>
> (C) Cross-referencing
>
> (D) Sorting and storing
>
> (E) Coding

You're looking for a step that does NOT belong in the procedure for preparing correspondence for filing. When people arrange and store business records according to a systematic plan, they do inspecting and indexing, cross-referencing, sorting and storing, and coding. Because they DON'T do date stamping at this time, (B) is the correct answer.

TIP It's easy to get confused while you're processing the information to answer a question with a LEAST, NOT, or EXCEPT in the question. If you treat the word "LEAST," "NOT," or "EXCEPT" as one of the details you must satisfy, you have a better chance of understanding what the question is asking. And when you check your answer, make "LEAST," "NOT," or "EXCEPT" one of the details you check for.

Be familiar with multiple-choice question types

Now that you have reviewed the basics of succeeding at multiple-choice questions, it should help to review the most common question formats you are likely to see.

1. Complete the statement

In this type of question, you are given an incomplete statement. You must select the choice that will make the completed statement correct.

> The federal act that declared the closed shop to be illegal is the
>
> (A) Landrum-Griffin Act
>
> (B) Norris-La Guardia Act
>
> (C) Taft-Hartley Act
>
> (D) Wagner Act
>
> (E) Robinson-Patman Act

To check your answer, reread the question and add your answer choice at the end. Be sure that your choice best completes the sentence. The correct answer is (C).

2. Which of the following

This question type is discussed in detail in a previous section. The question contains the details that must be satisfied for a correct answer, and it uses "which of the following" to limit the choices to the five choices shown, as this example demonstrates.

> Which of the following defines the word "byte" as used in information processing?
>
> (A) A unit of power
>
> (B) A machine for inputting data
>
> (C) A character of information
>
> (D) An on or off switch
>
> (E) A parity check

The correct answer is (C).

3. Roman numeral choices

This format is used when there can be more than one correct answer in the list. Consider the following example.

> An effective test to measure student achievement must possess which of the following characteristics?
>
> I. Reliability
> II. Validity
> III. Adaptability
>
> (A) I only
>
> (B) II only
>
> (C) III only
>
> (D) I and II only
>
> (E) II and III only

One useful strategy in this type of question is to assess each possible answer before looking at the answer choices, then evaluate the answer choices. In the question above, you need to apply your knowledge of teaching pedagogy and identify which of the three listed options is/are necessary for an effective test. You should be aware that an effective test must be reliable (Option I), in that the answers chosen to be correct have been researched and justified, so that a student who knows the material would answer them the same way if tested twice. It must also be valid (Option II), in that the questions chosen for the test match the objectives of instruction. Option III refers to the ability of the test to be altered or changed for a given circumstance. This may offer convenience for the instructor but does not make the measurement more effective. (D) specifies Options I and II only and, therefore, is the correct answer.

4. Questions containing LEAST, EXCEPT, NOT

This question type is discussed at length above. It asks you to select the choice that doesn't fit. You must be very careful with this question type, because it's easy to forget that you're selecting the negative. This question type is used in situations in which there are several good solutions, or ways to approach something, but also a clearly wrong way.

5. Other formats

New formats are developed from time to time in order to find new ways of assessing knowledge with multiple-choice questions. If you see a format you are not familiar with, read the directions carefully. Then read and approach the question the way you would any other question, asking yourself what you are supposed to be looking for, and what details are given in the question that help you find the answer.

Useful facts about the test

1. You can answer the questions in any order. You can go through the questions from beginning to end, as many test takers do, or you can create your own path. Perhaps you will want to answer questions in your strongest field first and then move from your strengths to your weaker areas. There is no right or wrong way. Use the approach that works for you.

2. There are no trick questions on the test. You don't have to find any hidden meanings or worry about trick wording. All of the questions on the test ask about subject matter knowledge in a straightforward manner.

3. Don't worry about answer patterns. There is one myth that says that answers on multiple-choice tests follow patterns. There is another myth that there will never be more than two questions with the same lettered answer following each other. There is no truth to either of these myths. Select the answer you think is correct, based on your knowledge of the subject.

4. There is no penalty for guessing. Your test score is based on the number of correct answers you have, and incorrect answers are not counted against you. When you don't know the answer to a question, try to eliminate any obviously wrong answers and then guess at the correct one.

5. It's OK to write in your test booklet. You can work problems right on the pages of the booklet, make notes to yourself, mark questions you want to review later, or write anything at all. Your test booklet will be destroyed after you are finished with it, so use it in any way that is helpful to you.

Smart tips for taking the test

1. Put your answers in the right "bubbles." It seems obvious, but be sure that you are "bubbling in" the answer to the right question on your answer sheet. A surprising number of candidates fill in a "bubble" without checking to see that the number matches the question they are answering.

2. Skip the questions you find to be extremely difficult. There are bound to be some questions that you think are hard. Rather than trying to answer these on your first pass through the test, leave them blank and mark them in your test booklet so that you can come back to them. Pay attention to the time as you answer the rest of the questions on the test and try to finish with 10 or 15 minutes remaining so that you can go back over the questions you left blank. Even if you don't know the answer the second time you read the questions, see whether you can narrow down the possible answers, and then guess.

3. Keep track of the time. Bring a watch to the test, just in case the clock in the test room is difficult for you to see. Remember that, on average, you have one minute to answer each of the 120 questions. One minute may not seem like much time, but you will be able to answer a number of questions in only a few seconds each. You will probably have plenty of time to answer all of the questions, but if you find yourself becoming bogged down by one or more questions, you might decide to move on and come back to that section later.

4. Read all of the possible answers before selecting one—and then reread the question to be sure the answer you have selected really answers the question being asked. Remember that a question that contains a phrase like "Which of the following does NOT…" is asking for the one answer that is NOT a correct statement or conclusion.

5. Check your answers. If you have extra time left over at the end of the test, look over each question and make sure that you have filled in the "bubble" on the answer sheet as you intended. Many candidates make careless mistakes that could have been corrected if they had checked their answers.

6. Don't worry about your score when you are taking the test. No one is expected to get all of the questions correct. Your score on this test is not analogous to your score on the SAT, the GRE, or other similar tests. It doesn't matter on this test whether you score very high or barely pass. If you meet the minimum passing scores for your state, and you meet the other requirements of the state for obtaining a teaching license, you will receive a license. Your actual score doesn't matter, as long as it is above the minimum required score. With your score report you will receive a booklet entitled *Understanding Your Praxis Scores*, which lists the passing scores for your state.

Chapter 5

Practice Questions for the *Business Education* Test

Now that you have studied the content topics and have worked through strategies relating to multiple-choice questions, you should take the following practice test. You will probably find it helpful to simulate actual testing conditions, giving yourself 100 minutes to work on the questions. You can cut out and use the answer sheet provided if you wish.

Keep in mind that the test you take at an actual administration will have different questions, although the proportion of questions in each area and major subarea will be approximately the same. You should not expect the percentage of questions you answer correctly in these practice questions to be exactly the same as when you take the test at an actual administration, since numerous factors affect a person's performance in any given testing situation.

When you have finished the practice questions, you can score your answers and read the explanations of the best answer choices in chapter 6.

Professional Assessments for Beginning Teachers ®

Business Education

Practice Questions

Time—100 Minutes
100 Questions

THE PRAXIS SERIES®
S E R I E S®
Professional Assessments for Beginning Teachers®

Answer Sheet C
PAGE 1

DO NOT USE INK

Use only a pencil with soft black lead (No. 2 or HB) to complete this answer sheet.
Be sure to fill in completely the oval that corresponds to the proper letter or number.
Completely erase any errors or stray marks.

1. NAME
Enter your last name and first initial.
Omit spaces, hyphens, apostrophes, etc.

Last Name (first 6 letters) | F I

2.

YOUR NAME:
(Print)

Last Name (Family or Surname) | First Name (Given) | M. I.

MAILING ADDRESS:
(Print)

P.O. Box or Street Address | Apt. # (if any)

City | State or Province

Country | Zip or Postal Code

TELEPHONE NUMBER: ( ) Home | ( ) Business

SIGNATURE:

TEST DATE:

6. TEST CENTER / REPORTING LOCATION

Center Number | Room Number

Center Name

City | State or Province

Country

5. CANDIDATE ID NUMBER

3. DATE OF BIRTH
Month | Day

Jan.
Feb.
Mar.
April
May
June
July
Aug.
Sept.
Oct.
Nov.
Dec.

4. SOCIAL SECURITY NUMBER

8. TEST BOOK SERIAL NUMBER

9. TEST FORM

10. TEST NAME

7. TEST CODE / FORM CODE

0
1

51055 • 08920 • TF71M500   Q2573-06
MH01159

I.N. 202974

Educational Testing Service, ETS, the ETS logo, and THE PRAXIS SERIES:PROFESSIONAL
ASSESSMENTS FOR BEGINNING TEACHERS are registered trademarks of
Educational Testing Service.

1 2 3 4

ⒺⓉⓈ

CERTIFICATION STATEMENT: (Please write the following statement below. DO NOT PRINT.)

"I hereby agree to the conditions set forth in the *Registration Bulletin* and certify that I am the person whose name and address appear on this answer sheet."

_____

_____

_____

SIGNATURE: _____   DATE: _____ / _____ / _____
                                                              Month   Day   Year

---

BE SURE EACH MARK IS DARK AND COMPLETELY FILLS THE INTENDED SPACE AS ILLUSTRATED HERE: ● .

1 Ⓐ Ⓑ Ⓒ Ⓓ	41 Ⓐ Ⓑ Ⓒ Ⓓ	81 Ⓐ Ⓑ Ⓒ Ⓓ	121 Ⓐ Ⓑ Ⓒ Ⓓ
2 Ⓐ Ⓑ Ⓒ Ⓓ	42 Ⓐ Ⓑ Ⓒ Ⓓ	82 Ⓐ Ⓑ Ⓒ Ⓓ	122 Ⓐ Ⓑ Ⓒ Ⓓ
3 Ⓐ Ⓑ Ⓒ Ⓓ	43 Ⓐ Ⓑ Ⓒ Ⓓ	83 Ⓐ Ⓑ Ⓒ Ⓓ	123 Ⓐ Ⓑ Ⓒ Ⓓ
4 Ⓐ Ⓑ Ⓒ Ⓓ	44 Ⓐ Ⓑ Ⓒ Ⓓ	84 Ⓐ Ⓑ Ⓒ Ⓓ	124 Ⓐ Ⓑ Ⓒ Ⓓ
5 Ⓐ Ⓑ Ⓒ Ⓓ	45 Ⓐ Ⓑ Ⓒ Ⓓ	85 Ⓐ Ⓑ Ⓒ Ⓓ	125 Ⓐ Ⓑ Ⓒ Ⓓ
6 Ⓐ Ⓑ Ⓒ Ⓓ	46 Ⓐ Ⓑ Ⓒ Ⓓ	86 Ⓐ Ⓑ Ⓒ Ⓓ	126 Ⓐ Ⓑ Ⓒ Ⓓ
7 Ⓐ Ⓑ Ⓒ Ⓓ	47 Ⓐ Ⓑ Ⓒ Ⓓ	87 Ⓐ Ⓑ Ⓒ Ⓓ	127 Ⓐ Ⓑ Ⓒ Ⓓ
8 Ⓐ Ⓑ Ⓒ Ⓓ	48 Ⓐ Ⓑ Ⓒ Ⓓ	88 Ⓐ Ⓑ Ⓒ Ⓓ	128 Ⓐ Ⓑ Ⓒ Ⓓ
9 Ⓐ Ⓑ Ⓒ Ⓓ	49 Ⓐ Ⓑ Ⓒ Ⓓ	89 Ⓐ Ⓑ Ⓒ Ⓓ	129 Ⓐ Ⓑ Ⓒ Ⓓ
10 Ⓐ Ⓑ Ⓒ Ⓓ	50 Ⓐ Ⓑ Ⓒ Ⓓ	90 Ⓐ Ⓑ Ⓒ Ⓓ	130 Ⓐ Ⓑ Ⓒ Ⓓ
11 Ⓐ Ⓑ Ⓒ Ⓓ	51 Ⓐ Ⓑ Ⓒ Ⓓ	91 Ⓐ Ⓑ Ⓒ Ⓓ	131 Ⓐ Ⓑ Ⓒ Ⓓ
12 Ⓐ Ⓑ Ⓒ Ⓓ	52 Ⓐ Ⓑ Ⓒ Ⓓ	92 Ⓐ Ⓑ Ⓒ Ⓓ	132 Ⓐ Ⓑ Ⓒ Ⓓ
13 Ⓐ Ⓑ Ⓒ Ⓓ	53 Ⓐ Ⓑ Ⓒ Ⓓ	93 Ⓐ Ⓑ Ⓒ Ⓓ	133 Ⓐ Ⓑ Ⓒ Ⓓ
14 Ⓐ Ⓑ Ⓒ Ⓓ	54 Ⓐ Ⓑ Ⓒ Ⓓ	94 Ⓐ Ⓑ Ⓒ Ⓓ	134 Ⓐ Ⓑ Ⓒ Ⓓ
15 Ⓐ Ⓑ Ⓒ Ⓓ	55 Ⓐ Ⓑ Ⓒ Ⓓ	95 Ⓐ Ⓑ Ⓒ Ⓓ	135 Ⓐ Ⓑ Ⓒ Ⓓ
16 Ⓐ Ⓑ Ⓒ Ⓓ	56 Ⓐ Ⓑ Ⓒ Ⓓ	96 Ⓐ Ⓑ Ⓒ Ⓓ	136 Ⓐ Ⓑ Ⓒ Ⓓ
17 Ⓐ Ⓑ Ⓒ Ⓓ	57 Ⓐ Ⓑ Ⓒ Ⓓ	97 Ⓐ Ⓑ Ⓒ Ⓓ	137 Ⓐ Ⓑ Ⓒ Ⓓ
18 Ⓐ Ⓑ Ⓒ Ⓓ	58 Ⓐ Ⓑ Ⓒ Ⓓ	98 Ⓐ Ⓑ Ⓒ Ⓓ	138 Ⓐ Ⓑ Ⓒ Ⓓ
19 Ⓐ Ⓑ Ⓒ Ⓓ	59 Ⓐ Ⓑ Ⓒ Ⓓ	99 Ⓐ Ⓑ Ⓒ Ⓓ	139 Ⓐ Ⓑ Ⓒ Ⓓ
20 Ⓐ Ⓑ Ⓒ Ⓓ	60 Ⓐ Ⓑ Ⓒ Ⓓ	100 Ⓐ Ⓑ Ⓒ Ⓓ	140 Ⓐ Ⓑ Ⓒ Ⓓ
21 Ⓐ Ⓑ Ⓒ Ⓓ	61 Ⓐ Ⓑ Ⓒ Ⓓ	101 Ⓐ Ⓑ Ⓒ Ⓓ	141 Ⓐ Ⓑ Ⓒ Ⓓ
22 Ⓐ Ⓑ Ⓒ Ⓓ	62 Ⓐ Ⓑ Ⓒ Ⓓ	102 Ⓐ Ⓑ Ⓒ Ⓓ	142 Ⓐ Ⓑ Ⓒ Ⓓ
23 Ⓐ Ⓑ Ⓒ Ⓓ	63 Ⓐ Ⓑ Ⓒ Ⓓ	103 Ⓐ Ⓑ Ⓒ Ⓓ	143 Ⓐ Ⓑ Ⓒ Ⓓ
24 Ⓐ Ⓑ Ⓒ Ⓓ	64 Ⓐ Ⓑ Ⓒ Ⓓ	104 Ⓐ Ⓑ Ⓒ Ⓓ	144 Ⓐ Ⓑ Ⓒ Ⓓ
25 Ⓐ Ⓑ Ⓒ Ⓓ	65 Ⓐ Ⓑ Ⓒ Ⓓ	105 Ⓐ Ⓑ Ⓒ Ⓓ	145 Ⓐ Ⓑ Ⓒ Ⓓ
26 Ⓐ Ⓑ Ⓒ Ⓓ	66 Ⓐ Ⓑ Ⓒ Ⓓ	106 Ⓐ Ⓑ Ⓒ Ⓓ	146 Ⓐ Ⓑ Ⓒ Ⓓ
27 Ⓐ Ⓑ Ⓒ Ⓓ	67 Ⓐ Ⓑ Ⓒ Ⓓ	107 Ⓐ Ⓑ Ⓒ Ⓓ	147 Ⓐ Ⓑ Ⓒ Ⓓ
28 Ⓐ Ⓑ Ⓒ Ⓓ	68 Ⓐ Ⓑ Ⓒ Ⓓ	108 Ⓐ Ⓑ Ⓒ Ⓓ	148 Ⓐ Ⓑ Ⓒ Ⓓ
29 Ⓐ Ⓑ Ⓒ Ⓓ	69 Ⓐ Ⓑ Ⓒ Ⓓ	109 Ⓐ Ⓑ Ⓒ Ⓓ	149 Ⓐ Ⓑ Ⓒ Ⓓ
30 Ⓐ Ⓑ Ⓒ Ⓓ	70 Ⓐ Ⓑ Ⓒ Ⓓ	110 Ⓐ Ⓑ Ⓒ Ⓓ	150 Ⓐ Ⓑ Ⓒ Ⓓ
31 Ⓐ Ⓑ Ⓒ Ⓓ	71 Ⓐ Ⓑ Ⓒ Ⓓ	111 Ⓐ Ⓑ Ⓒ Ⓓ	151 Ⓐ Ⓑ Ⓒ Ⓓ
32 Ⓐ Ⓑ Ⓒ Ⓓ	72 Ⓐ Ⓑ Ⓒ Ⓓ	112 Ⓐ Ⓑ Ⓒ Ⓓ	152 Ⓐ Ⓑ Ⓒ Ⓓ
33 Ⓐ Ⓑ Ⓒ Ⓓ	73 Ⓐ Ⓑ Ⓒ Ⓓ	113 Ⓐ Ⓑ Ⓒ Ⓓ	153 Ⓐ Ⓑ Ⓒ Ⓓ
34 Ⓐ Ⓑ Ⓒ Ⓓ	74 Ⓐ Ⓑ Ⓒ Ⓓ	114 Ⓐ Ⓑ Ⓒ Ⓓ	154 Ⓐ Ⓑ Ⓒ Ⓓ
35 Ⓐ Ⓑ Ⓒ Ⓓ	75 Ⓐ Ⓑ Ⓒ Ⓓ	115 Ⓐ Ⓑ Ⓒ Ⓓ	155 Ⓐ Ⓑ Ⓒ Ⓓ
36 Ⓐ Ⓑ Ⓒ Ⓓ	76 Ⓐ Ⓑ Ⓒ Ⓓ	116 Ⓐ Ⓑ Ⓒ Ⓓ	156 Ⓐ Ⓑ Ⓒ Ⓓ
37 Ⓐ Ⓑ Ⓒ Ⓓ	77 Ⓐ Ⓑ Ⓒ Ⓓ	117 Ⓐ Ⓑ Ⓒ Ⓓ	157 Ⓐ Ⓑ Ⓒ Ⓓ
38 Ⓐ Ⓑ Ⓒ Ⓓ	78 Ⓐ Ⓑ Ⓒ Ⓓ	118 Ⓐ Ⓑ Ⓒ Ⓓ	158 Ⓐ Ⓑ Ⓒ Ⓓ
39 Ⓐ Ⓑ Ⓒ Ⓓ	79 Ⓐ Ⓑ Ⓒ Ⓓ	119 Ⓐ Ⓑ Ⓒ Ⓓ	159 Ⓐ Ⓑ Ⓒ Ⓓ
40 Ⓐ Ⓑ Ⓒ Ⓓ	80 Ⓐ Ⓑ Ⓒ Ⓓ	120 Ⓐ Ⓑ Ⓒ Ⓓ	160 Ⓐ Ⓑ Ⓒ Ⓓ

FOR ETS USE ONLY	R1	R2	R3	R4	R5	R6	R7	R8	TR	CS

1. Which of the following groups would typically have voting rights in selecting a board of directors of a corporation?

   (A) Unionized employees
   (B) Senior employees
   (C) Common stockholders
   (D) Bondholders
   (E) Commercial creditors

2. The primary purpose of a tickler file is to

   (A) store telecommunication data
   (B) store canceled checks
   (C) store form paragraphs
   (D) design organizational charts
   (E) serve as a reminder system

3. In a computer-based business office, "what if" projections are usually made with the use of

   (A) a bar code reader
   (B) a communications software package
   (C) a database management software package
   (D) an electronic calendar
   (E) an electronic spreadsheet

4. Which of the following steps in organization development usually occurs first?

   (A) Intervention
   (B) Data collection
   (C) Implementation
   (D) Feedback
   (E) Evaluation

5. Which of the following typically qualifies a person for unemployment benefits?

   (A) Refusal to work
   (B) Discharge for misconduct
   (C) Involuntary termination
   (D) Inability to continue work
   (E) Voluntary termination

6. A truck that cost $8,500 is estimated to depreciate at the rate of 10 percent each year. If the declining-balance method of depreciation is used, the book value at the end of the second year is approximately

   (A) $1,615
   (B) $1,700
   (C) $6,800
   (D) $6,885
   (E) $7,650

7. A store or group of stores owned and controlled by the customers is most commonly called a

   (A) voluntary chain
   (B) one-line store
   (C) discount house
   (D) specialty shop
   (E) cooperative

8. Which of the following personal budget items is considered a variable expense?

   (A) Annual insurance premiums
   (B) Food
   (C) Real estate taxes
   (D) Loan payments for a car
   (E) Rental payments for a home

9. The actual rate of interest received on a savings account is called the

   (A) stated rate
   (B) periodic rate
   (C) effective rate
   (D) nominal rate
   (E) annual rate

10. Which of the following most accurately describes the function of the statute of frauds?

   (A) It categorizes the types of fraudulent contracts.
   (B) It outlines the characteristics of quasi-contracts.
   (C) It describes contracts that involve duress or undue influence.
   (D) It lists the kinds of contracts that must be in writing.
   (E) It explains the differences between formal and implied agreements.

11. A federal income tax payer should compare which of the following in order to decide whether or not to itemize deductions?

   (A) Adjustment deductions and total personal exemptions
   (B) Itemized deductions and adjustment deductions
   (C) Standard deductions and itemized deductions
   (D) Adjusted gross income and taxable income
   (E) Tax credits and itemized deductions

12. The interest charge on $2,000 borrowed for one year at a simple interest rate of 12% is

   (A) $100
   (B) $120
   (C) $144
   (D) $220
   (E) $240

13. Which of the following would be the LEAST appropriate basic bookkeeping/accounting concept to teach during the first week of an introductory course?

   (A) The bookkeeping/accounting equation
   (B) The opening balance sheet
   (C) The combined cash journal
   (D) The meaning of the terms "assets" and "proprietorship"
   (E) The meaning of the terms "debit" and "credit"

14.

Gross income	$30,000
Adjustments to income	$2,000
Itemized deductions	$6,500
Personal exemptions	$6,000
Standard deduction	$4,200

If itemized deductions are taken, the federal taxable income for the taxpayer whose income, deductions, and exemptions are listed above is

   (A) $11,300
   (B) $15,500
   (C) $17,800
   (D) $19,700
   (E) $23,200

15. If the same letter of application is to be sent to several prospective employers, each employer should ordinarily be sent

    (A) a faxed copy
    (B) an e-mailed copy
    (C) a photocopy
    (D) an individually handwritten copy by mail
    (E) an individually typewritten or keyboarded copy by mail

16. Typical features of a purely capitalist economy include which of the following?

    I.   Government ownership of the means of production
    II. Specialization of labor
    III. Competition in a free market

    (A) I only
    (B) III only
    (C) I and III only
    (D) II and III only
    (E) I, II, and III

17. Which of the following combinations of policies would the federal government most likely follow during a recession?

    (A) Increasing government spending and increasing the money supply
    (B) Decreasing government spending and increasing the money supply
    (C) Increasing taxes and increasing the money supply
    (D) Increasing taxes and decreasing the money supply
    (E) Decreasing taxes and decreasing the money supply

18.

Number	Item	Price	Extension
25	Chairs	$60.00	
10	Clocks	$10.00	
5	Lamps	$30.00	
10	Pictures	$20.00	
		TOTAL	

Value after the discount _____

After a discount of 10 percent for obsolescence, the total value of the inventory above is

    (A) $1,575
    (B) $1,755
    (C) $1,931
    (D) $1,950
    (E) $2,145

19. The two-letter state abbreviation accepted by the United States Postal Service for Missouri is

    (A) Mo
    (B) MO
    (C) Mi.
    (D) M.O.
    (E) MI

20. Which of the following eliminates the keyboarding of information by allowing typed documents to be scanned and the information contained in them to be transmitted to a word processor?

    (A) COM
    (B) OCR
    (C) CAR
    (D) CRT
    (E) CIM

21. Which of the following organizations would be most appropriate for a college senior who is a business education student?

    (A) Vocational Industrial Clubs of America
    (B) Distributive Education Clubs of America
    (C) Future Business Leaders of America
    (D) Phi Beta Lambda
    (E) Organizational Systems Research Association

22. The break-even point for a profit-oriented enterprise is achieved when

    (A) variable costs equal fixed costs
    (B) net revenue equals fixed costs
    (C) total revenue equals fixed costs
    (D) total revenue equals variable costs
    (E) total revenue equals total costs

23. Which of the following remedies would a buyer most likely seek when a seller breaches a contract and refuses to give up a unique gold coin?

    (A) Compensatory damages
    (B) Exemplary (punitive) damages
    (C) Nominal damages
    (D) Cancellation
    (E) Specific performance

24. The primary concern of subject-verb agreement is with

    (A) tense
    (B) gender
    (C) number
    (D) sentence structure
    (E) modification

25. All of the following are true of a database management system (DBMS) EXCEPT:

    (A) Storing, retrieving, sorting, and organizing large amounts of information are faster and easier than with a manual database.
    (B) A database is divided into files, records, and fields.
    (C) In establishing a database, a user should consider the fields of information needed and how much information those fields must contain.
    (D) All DBMS programs are equal in the amount of information that can be handled and the ease with which they can be used.
    (E) With a DBMS, a user can find and display specific information from the records by searching a file electronically for key words in a field.

26. Desktop publishing is dependent on which of the following basic components?

    (A) A card reader
    (B) A digital graphics scanner
    (C) Copy-compaction capacity
    (D) Decision-support software
    (E) Page-composition software

27. The Federal Reserve and its member banks are controlled by the

    (A) President of the United States
    (B) Board of Governors
    (C) Federal Trade Commission
    (D) member banks
    (E) Federal Deposit Insurance Corporation

28.

   I. Preparing the work sheet and statements
   II. Journalizing
   III. Posting
   IV. Preparing the post-closing trial balance
   V. Making the closing entries

   Which of the following is the correct order of the accounting cycle steps listed above?

   (A)   I, II, III, V, IV
   (B)   I, III, II, IV, V
   (C)   II, I, III, IV, V
   (D)   II, III, I, V, IV
   (E)   III, II, I, IV, V

29. Which of the following statements regarding dividends on common stock is true?

   (A)   They can be declared only in years in which the corporation earns a profit.
   (B)   They offset corporate income for federal tax purposes.
   (C)   They are the investors' sole incentive for purchasing stock in a corporation.
   (D)   They are typically declared as a specific amount per share.
   (E)   Their payment has priority over interest due on unsecured loans.

30. The national professional organization established primarily for business teachers at all levels of instruction is the

   (A)   National Business Education Association
   (B)   National Association for Business Education Teachers
   (C)   Association for Supervision and Curriculum Development
   (D)   American Vocational Association
   (E)   Future Business Leaders of America

31. Which of the following is designed primarily to produce text and graphics using varying print sizes, fonts, and images?

   (A)   Spreadsheet software
   (B)   Computer-aided design software
   (C)   Computer-graphics software
   (D)   Boilerplate software
   (E)   Desktop-publishing software

32. Which of the following practices is always acceptable when a statistical table is being typed?

   (A)   Double-spacing a primary heading of more than one line
   (B)   Aligning figures with decimals at the decimal point, when such figures appear in columns
   (C)   Capitalizing the first letter of each word in a secondary heading
   (D)   Centering a columnar heading over the first item in the column below it
   (E)   Double-spacing lines in the stub of the table

33. Which of the following can best be described as names and symbols that are used to identify a company and that are protected under the Lanham Act of 1946 when registered with the federal government?

   (A)   Patents
   (B)   Copyrights
   (C)   Testimonials
   (D)   Trademarks
   (E)   Endorsements

34. If an appliance store buys a refrigerator for $550 and sells it for $825, the percentage markup on cost is

   (A) 33 1/3%
   (B) 40%
   (C) 50%
   (D) 66 2/3%
   (E) 75%

35. The law of demand states that

   (A) a decline in the price of a good will tend to cause consumers to purchase more of that good
   (B) an increase in the price of a good will tend to cause consumers to purchase more of that good
   (C) an increase in the demand for a good will tend to cause the price of the good to decrease
   (D) a decrease in the demand for a good will tend to cause the price of the good to increase
   (E) an increase in consumer income will tend to cause an increase in consumer demand for a good

36. Which of the following types of insurance is designed to cover claims against a business for damages resulting from injuries to customers who suffer an accident in the place of business?

   (A) Business income
   (B) Extra expense
   (C) Liability
   (D) Group health and accident
   (E) Medical expense

37. Of the following, the term LEAST likely to be discussed in a course in retailing is

   (A) personal property
   (B) loss leaders
   (C) open-to-buy
   (D) price line
   (E) margin

38. When accounting students are learning how to analyze and record business transactions, which of the following should they be taught to consider first?

   (A) The amount of money to be recorded
   (B) The date of the transaction
   (C) The accounts that are affected
   (D) Whether the accounts are increased or decreased
   (E) Whether the accounts are to be debited or credited

39. The major long-range goal of production keyboarding is to have students learn to key which of the following?

   (A) Problem-type material at three-fourths the straight-copy rate
   (B) Finished copy from unarranged copy according to acceptable work standards
   (C) Drill exercises at a rate of 60 words per minute
   (D) Production problems for five minutes without error
   (E) Straight copy at rapid rates for sustained periods of time

40. True statements about the information in both random-access memory (RAM) and read-only memory (ROM) include which of the following?

I. It is lost when the power to the computer is turned off.
II. It can be altered by the user.
III. It can include instructions as well as data.
IV. It can be read by the CPU.

(A) IV only
(B) I and III only
(C) II and III only
(D) III and IV only
(E) II, III, and IV only

41. Which of the following expenses would be classified as a selling expense?

(A) Salaries paid to office workers
(B) Fees paid to credit card companies by the seller
(C) Depreciation on a building
(D) Interest paid on capital improvements
(E) Expenditures for utilities

42. When a stockholder signs a proxy solicited by the management of a corporation, the stockholder has authorized the management to

(A) issue additional shares to the stockholder
(B) repurchase the stockholder's shares
(C) call in the stockholder's shares of preferred stock
(D) vote the stockholder's shares
(E) convert the stockholder's preferred stock issues to common stock

43. When the totals of the trial balance are equal, the accountant knows that

(A) all journal entries have been posted to the correct ledger accounts
(B) all original entries were made correctly
(C) the company has made a reasonable amount of profit
(D) equal amounts of debits and credits have been posted
(E) no errors have been made in determining account balances

44. The national debt of the United States can best be defined as the

(A) annual deficit created by an excess of government spending over tax receipts
(B) accumulated sum of deficits minus surpluses of the federal government
(C) amount owed by United States companies to foreign governments
(D) social and economic costs created by social welfare programs
(E) total consumer debt of residents of the United States

45. A consignment is a bailment for which of the following?

(A) Safekeeping
(B) Hiring
(C) Work and services
(D) Sales purposes
(E) Banking and insurance

46. Most businesses in the United States are organized as

(A) corporations
(B) joint ventures
(C) limited partnerships
(D) partnerships
(E) sole proprietorships

47. Which of the following is an interlinked system of computers designed to allow for the mutual exchange of information?

(A) OCR
(B) CRT
(C) RBG
(D) LAN
(E) ROM

48. If a business firm pays $1,000 for furniture on account, which of the following statements about journal entries made for the transaction is true?

(A) Cash should be credited; Office Furniture should be debited.
(B) Office Expense should be debited; Accounts Payable should be credited.
(C) Office Furniture should be debited; Accounts Payable should be credited.
(D) Accounts Payable and Office Furniture should be debited; Cash and the individual payable account should be credited.
(E) No asset accounts should be affected by the transaction, since it was on account.

49. It is appropriate for an applicant for a job to discuss all of the following topics at the interview EXCEPT the

(A) salary being offered
(B) applicant's personal strengths
(C) fact that the applicant has researched the company
(D) aspects of a previous employer that the applicant disliked
(E) potential for advancement

50. Which of the following would be classified as Other Income on an income statement?

(A) Sales Discount
(B) Merchandise Inventory
(C) Purchases Returns and Allowances
(D) Sales Returns and Allowances
(E) Interest Earned

51. Federal funds for business education have tended mostly to support which of the following areas?

(A) Consumer education
(B) Economics instruction
(C) Personal-use skills
(D) Personal development
(E) Vocational skills

52. The gross domestic product (GDP) can be defined as the

    (A) monetary value of all final goods and services produced in a given year

    (B) monetary value of all economic resources used in production in a given year

    (C) monetary value of all capital gains minus liabilities incurred in a given year

    (D) national income minus all nonincome charges against output in a given year

    (E) total expenditures of federal, state, and local governments in a given year

53. Which of the following most accurately describes a macro in information processing?

    (A) A grammar and style checker for verifying correct construction of sentences, word usage, and nonsexist language

    (B) Two or more functions that may be viewed at the same time on the screen

    (C) A program capable of importing and exporting text, graphics, voice, and video

    (D) A header or footer that is inserted into text

    (E) Stored keystrokes for frequently used functions that can be accessed with only one or two keystrokes

54. Which of the following represents a full block-style business letter?

    (A)   (B)   (C)   (D)   (E)

55. Which of the following is an advantage of floppy disks over hard disks in a personal computer system?

    (A) Greater storage capacity per disk

    (B) Faster access to data

    (C) Longer useful life

    (D) Lower cost per disk

    (E) Less maintenance required

56. A drastic decrease in oil prices would most likely have which of the following effects on the United States economy?

    (A) Reduced inflation and stimulated economic growth

    (B) Increased inflation and reduced economic growth

    (C) Increased inflation and stimulated economic growth

    (D) Reduced inflation and reduced economic growth

    (E) Increased inflation and reduced level of unemployment

57. Which of the following functions is NOT generally associated with the responsibilities of a financial manager?

    (A) Treasurer

    (B) Comptroller

    (C) Producer

    (D) Accountant

    (E) Bookkeeper

58. According to research, the competency most needed at entry for success in most business occupations today is

    (A) computer literacy
    (B) communication skills
    (C) records management
    (D) mail management
    (E) time management

59. In a cooperative office-education program, the major goal is to help the students to

    (A) develop the ability to transfer what they have learned at school to the job and vice versa
    (B) understand the importance of good work habits in the maintenance of a smooth-running business
    (C) learn to work without requiring close supervision
    (D) obtain a job closely related to their major fields of study
    (E) see the relationship of work to their own earning potential

60. Vance, the owner of a clothing store, advised Julia, the store manager, to use her best judgment when picking merchandise for the store. Vance's only caution was, "Do not buy designer jeans." Later, Julia did purchase a line of designer jeans from Casual Wear, Inc., but they did not sell, causing a large inventory buildup. Casual Wear had no knowledge of Vance's directive to Julia not to buy designer jeans. Vance refused to pay, and Casual Wear sued for the purchase price. In this situation, Vance is NOT relieved from liability to pay for the jeans purchased by Julia because Julia

    (A) had express authority to purchase the jeans
    (B) had implied authority to purchase the jeans
    (C) had apparent authority to purchase the jeans
    (D) was an undisclosed principal
    (E) can claim *respondeat superior*

61. The underlying premise of competency-based programs in business education is that

    (A) objectives should direct instruction
    (B) students are evaluated in relation to their peers
    (C) mastery of all competencies is necessary for entry-level employment
    (D) objectives need not be shared with students
    (E) objectives should be broad enough to allow for individual interpretation

62. A retailer who prices a shirt at $24.95 rather than $25.00 is most likely using a strategy known as

    (A) discount pricing
    (B) odd pricing
    (C) prestige pricing
    (D) differential pricing
    (E) list pricing

63. The search function in word processing is designed to locate

    (A) spelling errors in a text
    (B) a file on a data disk
    (C) a character or a set of characters in a text
    (D) the source of a document on a data disk
    (E) a synonym for a word in a text

64. The major focus of vocational business education programs should be

   (A)   training a sufficient number of qualified students to meet local labor requirements
   (B)   being well informed about and teaching toward the needs of the business community
   (C)   offering computer-literacy training at all levels
   (D)   coordinating keyboarding instruction at the elementary level
   (E)   providing placement services for successful students

65. A person who endorses a paycheck by simply signing his or her name on the back of the check is making a

   (A)   qualified endorsement
   (B)   restrictive endorsement
   (C)   licensed endorsement
   (D)   blank endorsement
   (E)   full endorsement

66. In cooperative education, the individualized statement of work to be done, which serves as a guide for on-the-job instruction and in-school instruction, is called a

   (A)   training plan
   (B)   competency program
   (C)   work schedule
   (D)   job guide
   (E)   job description

67. Which of the following is defined as an entity's total assets minus its total liabilities?

   (A)   Accounts receivable
   (B)   Net worth
   (C)   Operating expenses
   (D)   Cash receipts
   (E)   Marginal profit

68. During a period of increasing prices, the use of the FIFO method of valuing inventory rather than the LIFO method will result in

   (A)   higher gross revenue
   (B)   reduced fixed costs
   (C)   a lower inventory valuation
   (D)   a lower reported net income
   (E)   a lower cost of merchandise sold

69. Objective tests in secretarial subjects are best used to measure

   (A)   interpersonal skills
   (B)   the ability to think independently
   (C)   the ability to perform receptionists' duties
   (D)   growth in self-expression
   (E)   knowledge gained

70. Which of the following is the most important outcome for a student completing a business education curriculum?

   (A)   Awareness of business technology skills
   (B)   Knowledge of personal investing concepts
   (C)   Attainment of both business skills and knowledge
   (D)   Identification and operation of several types of computers
   (E)   Identification of economic trends

71. Which of the following is a legal requirement if a person wishes to obtain property insurance and be eligible for compensation for any loss?

    (A) Self-insurance
    (B) Insurable interest
    (C) Coinsurance
    (D) Speculative risk
    (E) Comprehensive insurance

72. Which of the following teaching techniques would be best to use when teaching special needs students in business education?

    (A) Lecturing on the importance of good study habits
    (B) Encouraging students to compete with their peers
    (C) Using abstract examples and illustrations
    (D) Providing repetition and review of lessons
    (E) Giving frequent unit tests

73. Which of the following is an employee salary reduction that is, by law, matched by the employer?

    (A) Federal income tax
    (B) State income tax
    (C) State unemployment tax
    (D) FICA tax
    (E) Workers' compensation premiums

74. The main objective of advanced instructional units on the income statement and balance sheet is to teach students to

    (A) identify debits and credits
    (B) balance the statements easily
    (C) use proper business form
    (D) categorize each account
    (E) analyze and interpret the information

75. A balance sheet is best described as a

    (A) flow statement listing net worth and sources of income
    (B) flow statement listing sources of income and expenditures
    (C) condition statement noting assets and claims against the assets
    (D) condition statement noting assets and incomes
    (E) condition statement noting liabilities and expenditures

76. Arranging information in a document in order to make it more attractive and easier to use and read is called

    (A) compiling
    (B) categorizing
    (C) ranking
    (D) sorting
    (E) formatting

77. The primary objective in public speaking is to

    (A) reconcile
    (B) define
    (C) analyze
    (D) persuade
    (E) criticize

78. Which of the following formulas is used to calculate a firm's merchandise inventory turnover?

  (A) Cost of goods sold divided by beginning inventory
  (B) Cost of goods sold divided by ending inventory
  (C) Cost of goods sold divided by average inventory
  (D) Average inventory divided by cost of goods sold
  (E) Ending inventory divided by beginning inventory

79. The market value of a share of common stock is equal to the

  (A) book value of the stock
  (B) par value of the stock
  (C) current price at which the stock is trading
  (D) liquidating value of the stock
  (E) issuing price of the stock less the par value

80. In most cases, if there is a need for a new business to continue beyond the life of its owner or owners, the business should be organized as a

  (A) corporation
  (B) cooperative
  (C) limited partnership
  (D) general partnership
  (E) sole proprietorship

81. Which of the following is included in the United States Postal Service category of second-class mail?

  (A) Greeting cards in unsealed envelopes
  (B) Packages weighing less than 8 ounces
  (C) Packages conveyed within the same postal zone
  (D) Advertisements and other similar printed material
  (E) Newspapers and periodicals

82. Bar codes that are used as input to a computer system for pricing and inventory control are also known as

  (A) UPC symbols
  (B) VDT symbols
  (C) CRT symbols
  (D) CPM symbols
  (E) CPU symbols

83. Data that must be retrieved electronically, randomly, and quickly is best stored on

  (A) magnetic tape
  (B) microfiche
  (C) punched cards
  (D) punched paper tape
  (E) hard or floppy disks

84. When the sender of an important document wishes to have proof that the document has been delivered to a specified destination, the sender can use which of the following methods offered by the United States Postal Service?

  (A) Certified mail
  (B) Insured mail
  (C) Special-delivery mail
  (D) First-class mail
  (E) Airmail

85. If a nation begins importing more goods and its exports remain constant, it will experience an increase in

    (A) the value of its currency
    (B) the number of foreign markets for its products
    (C) the outflow of its currency
    (D) inflation
    (E) employment

86. Which of the following approaches to business education curriculums is LEAST consistent with current job-market trends?

    (A) Concentration on job-specific office training
    (B) Concern for the impact of technology on job responsibilities of office workers
    (C) Emphasis on broad transferable skills for both employment and personal use
    (D) Critical emphasis on analytical thinking skills
    (E) Strategies for American business to deal successfully with international competition

87. The terms of a $3,000 sale on June 1 were 2/10, n/30. If payment was made on June 9, the debtor received a discount of what, if any, amount?

    (A) $400
    (B) $60
    (C) $40
    (D) $6
    (E) $0

88. All of the following are typical duties of a receptionist EXCEPT

    (A) arranging meetings
    (B) making routine decisions
    (C) performing clerical duties
    (D) planning budgets
    (E) keeping daily logs

89. All of the following are functions of the Federal Reserve System EXCEPT

    (A) regulating the money supply
    (B) implementing federal tax law
    (C) supervising member banks
    (D) providing a system of check collection and clearing
    (E) supplying the economy with paper currency

90. A personal-computer factory has fixed costs of $10,000 and variable costs of $200 per unit. How many units must be sold at $1,200 for the factory to earn a profit of $10,000 ?

    (A) 17
    (B) 20
    (C) 25
    (D) 40
    (E) 100

91. All of the following are examples of proper telephone techniques for an office worker EXCEPT

    (A) making each caller welcome by using the caller's name in the conversation
    (B) making the call as short as possible for efficiency
    (C) answering each call on the first or second ring
    (D) giving the appropriate forwarding number before transferring a call
    (E) continuing the task in process while answering the telephone call

92. Which of the following is NOT an element of marketing mix?

    (A) Product
    (B) Price
    (C) Communication
    (D) Competition
    (E) Distribution

93. In developing basic keyboarding skills, a teacher should place greatest emphasis on student behavioral objectives related to the

    (A) knowledge level of the cognitive domain
    (B) comprehension level of the cognitive domain
    (C) synthesis level of the cognitive domain
    (D) characterization level of the affective domain
    (E) perception level of the psychomotor domain

94. To be ethical, a business must do all of the following EXCEPT

    (A) refrain from selling goods and services that are injurious to health
    (B) refrain from misrepresentation
    (C) give customers good value for their money
    (D) stand behind its goods following a sale
    (E) develop adequate customer-service policies

95. Which of the following information sources is commonly used for journal entries?

    (A) Beginning inventory
    (B) Cost of goods sold
    (C) Invoices
    (D) Checking account balance
    (E) Requisitions

96. A basic-word processing software program is LEAST likely to perform which of the following?

    (A) Permit spelling changes in a document
    (B) Search for and replace words
    (C) Locate errors in word choice
    (D) Move paragraphs from one page to another
    (E) Number pages of text automatically

97. Under the Uniform Commercial Code, an instrument that is negotiable must

    (A) be in writing on a standard form
    (B) contain a conditional promise to pay a definite amount of money
    (C) be payable on demand or at a definite time
    (D) be payable in goods
    (E) specify a rate of interest to be paid

98. The LEAST important factor in selecting equipment for a business education classroom is being sure that the equipment will

   (A) further the aim of business education in the school
   (B) fill the curriculum needs of the school
   (C) be the kind used in the business community
   (D) be the one with which the instructor is most familiar
   (E) be up-to-date and come with a service contract

99. Title to goods purchased passes to the retailer at the time the merchandise is delivered to the carrier when it is sent in which of the following ways?

   (A) F.O.B. Shipping Point
   (B) F.O.B./P.O.E.
   (C) F.O.B. Destination
   (D) F.O.B. Purchase on Consignment
   (E) F.O.B./C.O.D.

100. All of the following types of communication services are based on electronic dissemination EXCEPT

   (A) telex
   (B) facsimile
   (C) express mail
   (D) local area network
   (E) bulletin-board service

Chapter 6

Right Answers and Explanations for the Practice
Questions for the *Business Education* Test

Now that you have answered all of the practice questions, you can check your work. Compare your answers with the correct answers in the table below.

Question Number	Correct Answer	Content Category	Question Number	Correct Answer	Content Category
1	C	United States Economic Systems	30	A	Professional Business Education
2	E	Office Procedures and Management, Communications, and Employability Skills	31	E	Processing Information
3	E	Business and Its Environment	32	B	Business and Its Environment
4	B	Business and Its Environment	33	D	Business and Its Environment
5	C	Business and Its Environment	34	C	Money Management
6	D	Accounting and Marketing	35	A	United States Economic Systems
7	E	United States Economic Systems	36	C	Business and Its Environment
8	B	Money Management	37	A	Accounting and Marketing
9	C	Money Management	38	C	Accounting and Marketing
10	D	Business and Its Environment	39	B	Processing Information
11	C	United States Economic Systems	40	D	Processing Information
12	E	Money Management	41	B	Accounting and Marketing
13	C	Professional Business Education	42	D	Money Management
14	B	Money Management	43	D	Accounting and Marketing
15	E	Office Procedures and Management, Communications, and Employability Skills	44	B	United States Economic Systems
16	D	United States Economic Systems	45	D	Business and Its Environment
17	A	United States Economic Systems	46	E	United States Economic Systems
18	B	Money Management	47	D	Processing Information
19	B	Office Procedures and Management, Communications, and Employability Skills	48	C	Accounting and Marketing
20	B	Processing Information	49	D	Office Procedures and Management, Communications, and Employability Skills
21	D	Professional Business Education	50	E	Accounting and Marketing
22	E	Money Management	51	E	Professional Business Education
23	E	Business and Its Environment	52	A	United States Economic Systems
24	C	Office Procedures and Management, Communications, and Employability Skills	53	E	Processing Information
25	D	Processing Information	54	A	Processing Information
26	E	Processing Information	55	D	Processing Information
27	B	United States Economic Systems	56	A	United States Economic Systems
28	D	Accounting and Marketing	57	C	Business and Its Environment
29	D	Money Management	58	B	Professional Business Education

59	A	Professional Business Education
60	C	Business and Its Environment
61	A	Professional Business Education
62	B	Accounting and Marketing
63	C	Processing Information
64	B	Professional Business Education
65	D	Business and Its Environment
66	A	Professional Business Education
67	B	Accounting and Marketing
68	E	Accounting and Marketing
69	E	Professional Business Education
70	C	Professional Business Education
71	B	Business and Its Environment
72	D	Professional Business Education
73	D	United States Economic Systems
74	E	Professional Business Education
75	C	Accounting and Marketing
76	E	Processing Information
77	D	Office Procedures and Management, Communications, and Employability Skills
78	C	Money Management
79	C	Money Management

80	A	United States Economic Systems
81	E	Office Procedures and Management, Communications, and Employability Skills
82	A	Processing Information
83	E	Processing Information
84	A	Office Procedures and Management, Communications, and Employability Skills
85	C	United States Economic Systems
86	A	Professional Business Education
87	B	Money Management
88	D	Office Procedures and Management, Communications, and Employability Skills
89	B	United States Economic Systems
90	B	Money Management
91	E	Office Procedures and Management, Communications, and Employability Skills
92	D	Accounting and Marketing
93	E	Professional Business Education
94	E	Business and Its Environment
95	C	Accounting and Marketing
96	C	Processing Information
97	C	Business and Its Environment
98	D	Professional Business Education
99	A	Business and Its Environment
100	C	Office Procedures and Management, Communications, and Employability Skills

Explanations of Right Answers

1. This question asks you to determine who has the rights to vote for a corporate board of directors. Common stockholders are eligible to vote for the board of directors since stockholders are actually the owners of the corporation. (C) is the only choice that pertains to stockholders, thus making it the only correct choice.

2. This question tests your knowledge of records management procedures. A tickler file is a folder that consists of many different pockets representing the days of the month. Important information for each day is placed in the appropriate section, thus serving as a reminder to complete a particular activity. Since it is a reminder system, (E) is the correct answer.

3. This question tests your understanding of the use of spreadsheets. Electronic spreadsheets are designed to allow the user to create formulas that will produce a desired result. Those same formulas can be used to project additional data by creating "what if" scenarios. As the projected input is changed, the results change, thus allowing you to examine the outcome if that set of data is used. (E) is the correct answer.

4. This question asks you to apply your knowledge of business planning. In the creation of an effective plan, data collection must be the first consideration. The results of the data collected will determine how to implement the plan, thus providing for the necessary intervention and evaluation that are necessary. Data collection is always the first step in organization development; thus (B) is the correct answer.

5. This question asks you to apply principles of business and consumer law. Unemployment benefits are reserved for only those employees who are terminated from their job involuntarily, through no fault of their own. If the employee is unable to work, the employee is eligible for disability, not unemployment benefits. Therefore, the correct answer to this question is (C).

6. This question tests your knowledge of the declining balance method of depreciation. Since declining balance is an accelerated depreciation method, higher amounts of depreciation are taken in earlier years. Thus, at the end of the **first** year, the book value would be $7,650, calculated as follows: ($8,500 - [$8,500 x 0.10]). At the end of the **second** year the book value would be $6,885, calculated as follows: ($7,650 - [$7,650 x 0.10]). Therefore, (D) is the correct answer.

7. This question tests your understanding of the forms of business organization. Customers who join together to own and manage a store or group of stores are known as a cooperative. None of the other choices indicated in this question provide for that control and management by the customers themselves. The answer to this question, therefore, is (E).

8. This question tests your understanding of the concepts of personal budgeting. Variable expenses fluctuate from month to month. Insurance, taxes, loan payments, and rent are all

constant expenses. Food costs, however, change each time you shop and therefore are variable expenses, making (B) the correct answer.

9. This question tests your understanding of finance terminology. Interest on a savings account is compounded as the year passes; therefore the printed rate differs from the actual, or effective, rate. (C), therefore, is correct.

10. This question tests your knowledge of business law. By definition the Statute of Frauds requires that certain types of transactions be evidenced in writing in order to be binding or enforceable. Since none of the other choices pertain to those written contract choices, letter (D) is the correct answer.

11. This question tests your understanding of taxation. Each taxpayer is allocated a particular amount of standard deduction. If the taxpayer is able to demonstrate that the itemized deductions are greater than the standard deduction, then the itemized figure can be used. Therefore, (C) is correct.

12. This question tests your knowledge of how to calculate simple interest. Simple interest is calculated by multiplying the principal times the rate of interest. Since $2,000 x 0.12 equals $240, (E) is the correct answer.

13. This question tests your understanding of teaching strategies. It is very important that introductory accounting instruction build a solid basic foundation in the beginning weeks

of the course. The combined cash journal is a topic that should be presented much later in the curriculum. The correct answer is (C).

14. This question tests your knowledge of the mathematics of calculating taxes. The correct calculation to compute taxable income is

Gross income	$30,000
Adjustment to income	- 2,000
Personal exemptions	- 6,000
Itemized deductions	- 6,500
Taxable income	$15,500

The correct answer is (B)

15. This question tests your understanding of written communications. Letters of application are a request for possible employment. It is very important that each letter be individually prepared in order to indicate genuine interest in possible employment to a potential employer. Unless the employer specifically requests otherwise, mail (rather than e-mail or fax) is the appropriate way to send the letter. The correct answer, therefore, is (E).

16. This question asks you to use your knowledge of the free enterprise system. Under a pure capitalist economy, the government does not own the various means of production. Competition and specialization of labor are two core fundamentals of a pure capitalist economy. Therefore, (D) is the correct answer.

17. This question tests your understanding of government and banking policies. A recession is a period of falling demand and lower interest rates. Generally, during a recession, the unemployment rate increases because the demand for goods is depressed. Any increase in taxes would further reduce consumer spending. Increasing the money supply would have the effect of increased employment, since more money would be available to the consumer for spending. Therefore, (A) is the correct answer.

18. This question asks you to use your knowledge of how to calculate total inventory after a discount is applied. In order to complete this problem, you must first calculate each extension by multiplying the number of items times the price for each item of inventory. Then you multiply the **total** by 0.90 (100% - the 10% discount) to calculate the value after the discount. The correct answer is (B).

19. This question tests your recall of the correct two-letter state abbreviations. According to the United States Postal Service, all state abbreviations must be two uppercase letters with no punctuation. The correct two letters for Missouri are MO. The correct answer for this question is (B).

20. This question tests your understanding of information-processing concepts. OCR stands for optical character recognition. An OCR reader is a device used to scan documents into a word processor. The correct answer, therefore, is (B).

21. This question tests your knowledge of student organizations. Only two of the organizations listed are offered at the college level. Distributive Education Clubs of America is, in addition to having the same name at the high school level, the college-level student organization for marketing students. Phi Beta Lambda is the college-level student organization for business students. Therefore, (D) is the correct answer for this question.

22. This question tests your understanding of financial management data. (A) through (D) are incorrect choices because they are not comparing data that are considered similar in source or result. The break-even point is the point at which the **total** costs match the **total** revenues. Therefore, (E) is the correct answer.

23. This question tests your knowledge of contract law. Since the item purchased was a unique item and was still in the possession of the seller, the only remedy would be to have the coin delivered to the buyer. This is specific performance; therefore, the answer is (E).

24. This question tests your understanding of business English principles. The subject and verb must always agree in **number** in order for the sentence to be correct. For example, it is inappropriate to say "The cows is in the barn." The correct wording is "The cows are in the barn." The subject and verb must agree in number. The correct answer is (C).

25. This question tests your knowledge of the use of database systems. (A), (B), and (E) are clearly all accurate descriptions of the nature and function of a database. (C) describes part of the correct procedures for establishing a database. Only (D) is incorrect, since database management programs are clearly unequal in both their ease of use and amount of information handled. The correct answer, therefore, is (D).

26. This question tests your knowledge of desktop publishing concepts. Desktop publishing is defined as pre-press publishing operations completed with desktop computers. In order to successfully complete desktop published items, you must effectively utilize page-composition software. The correct answer is (E).

27. This question tests your understanding of the Federal Reserve System. The Federal Reserve System is comprised of twelve Federal Reserve Banks and many member banks throughout the country. This system of banking is controlled by the Federal Reserve's Board of Governors. Therefore, (B) is the correct answer.

28. This question tests your understanding of accounting concepts. The basic accounting cycle consists of journalizing each entry, then posting it. Preparing the work sheet and statements is the next step, followed by the closing entries and the preparation of the post-closing trial balance. (D) is the correct answer.

29. This question tests your knowledge of stocks and investments. Common stock is considered the most basic element of corporate ownership. A dividend is a percentage of net income that is distributed to each shareholder according to the amount of the investment. These payments are typically declared as a specific amount per share. Therefore, (D) is the correct answer.

30. This question asks you to apply your knowledge of professional organizations. (C) and (D) are nationally recognized teacher organizations, but not primarily for business education teachers as specified in the question. (E) is a national student organization and thus is incorrect. (B) does not exist, due to the incorrect ordering of the words. (A) is therefore the correct answer.

31. This question asks you to determine which type of software is designed primarily to produce text and graphics. Spreadsheet software is designed primarily to manipulate numbers and calculate numeric data using numeric input. Computer-aided design software is used primarily to produce architectural or engineering drawings and designs. Computer-graphics software is primarily used to produce graphical images but does not utilize much text. Boilerplates are templates; therefore boilerplate software must refer to software designed primarily as a template for other work. Desktop-publishing software allows the user to produce text and graphics in varying sizes and images. Therefore, (E) is the correct answer.

32. This question asks you to use your knowledge of setting up and keying statistical tables. (A) is incorrect because headings of more than one line are single-spaced in a document. (C) is incorrect because in a secondary heading only certain words are capitalized. (D) is incorrect because column headings are centered over the longest item in the column, not necessarily the first item in the column. (E) is incorrect. Double-spacing the body of the table is not always an acceptable format. Single-spacing is preferred. (B) is the correct answer. You should always align figures within tables at the decimal point when setting tabs and keying.

33. This question tests your knowledge of legal issues involving marketing. The Lanham Act of 1946 specifically addresses United States trademark laws. (D) is the correct answer.

34. This question asks you to calculate markup based on cost expressed as a percentage. To find the markup rate based on cost, you must divide the amount of markup by the cost price. In this problem, you must calculate the amount of markup by subtracting the cost ($550) from the selling price ($825). The markup is, therefore, $275. You must then divide $275 by $550 in order to obtain the percentage markup based on cost. The correct answer is (C).

35. This question asks you to apply your knowledge of marketing essentials and the laws of supply and demand. (B) is incorrect because consumers do not purchase more when prices are higher. (C) is also incorrect because when demand increases, so does price.

(D) is incorrect because decreases in demand cause decreases in price. (E) is incorrect as well because increases in consumer income do not have a bearing on the laws of supply and demand. (A) is the classic law of supply and demand. (A) is the correct answer.

36. This question asks you to apply your knowledge of insurance under the topic of business law. Liability insurance coverage protects a person or business against lawsuits arising from both property damage and/or bodily injury. In the scenario stated, liability insurance would cover a claim resulting from a customer suffering an accident in a place of business. (C) is therefore the correct answer. (A), (B), and (E) are not types of insurance and are therefore incorrect. (D) is an insurance plan offered by an employer to a group of employees for specific coverages and is also an incorrect answer.

37. This question tests your understanding of curricular topics in marketing. Personal property issues would be more likely to be discussed in a business law class rather than a marketing class. The correct answer, therefore, is (A).

38. This question asks you to recognize one of the basic rules of beginning accounting. (D) and (E) are considered after it has been decided which accounts are affected. (A) and (B) are clerical issues when the actual transaction is recorded. (C) is the first consideration when analyzing and recording business transactions and therefore is the correct answer.

39. This question asks you to apply your knowledge of teaching keyboarding. The primary goal of keyboarding instruction is for the learner to key a job in unarranged format and produce a mailable document that complies with current standards. (A), (C), (D), and (E), are all incorrect because they state that the rate at which keying is completed is the long-range goal of keyboarding. Accuracy takes precedence over speed, so (B) is the correct answer.

40. This question asks you to recognize computer terminology and apply your knowledge. Random-access memory (RAM) is lost when power to the computer is turned off. Read-only memory is retained when the computer is turned off. Therefore, statement I cannot apply to both. RAM can be altered by the user, but ROM cannot, so statement II is not true for both. Statements III and IV are both true statements regarding RAM and ROM. Therefore, (D) is the correct answer to the question.

41. This question tests your knowledge of accounting concepts. For an expense to qualify as a selling expense, it must be directly related to the sale of the product. Office worker salaries, depreciation, capital improvement interest, and utilities are not expenses related directly to the sale of the product. The correct answer, (B), is the only expense that is directly connected with the sale of the product.

42. This question tests your knowledge of finance and investing. A proxy, by definition, is a written authorization by a shareholder to another person to vote the stock owned by the shareholder. It does not provide for the issuing of additional shares, repurchasing of shares, converting of shares, or calling in of shares. (D) is the correct answer.

43. This question tests your knowledge of basic accounting concepts. The purpose of the trial balance is to prove that all entries have been posted equally to the debit and credit sides of the affected accounts. Therefore, (D) is the correct answer.

44. This question tests your understanding of banking and governmental fiscal policy. The national debt is the amount of money that the U.S. government spends in excess of its income. It is calculated by subtracting the surplus of the federal government from its accumulated deficit. (B) is correct.

45. This question asks you to apply your knowledge of business law terminology. A bailment is defined as the temporary possession by one person of another person's goods. Goods purchased on consignment reflect temporary ownership. Therefore, both terms are related to marketing and selling, making (D) the correct answer. (A), (B), (C) and (E) have nothing to do with ownership or possession of goods.

46. This question asks you to apply your knowledge of business organizations. (A), (B), (C) and (D) are all valid types of business organizations. Sole proprietorships, however, are the most common form of business ownership in the United States. (E) is the correct answer.

47. This question asks you to apply your knowledge of basic computer terminology (acronyms). (A) stands for optical character recognition and is used for input purposes. This answer is incorrect. (B) refers to a monitor or screen and is incorrect. (C) stands for red-blue-green and refers to a monitor or screen, also incorrect. (E) stands for read-only memory and is incorrect. (D) stands for local area network and by definition is an interlinked system of computers designed for communication. Therefore, (D) is the correct answer.

48. This question tests your knowledge of accounting concepts. The two accounts that are involved with this transaction are Office Furniture, an asset account, and Accounts Payable, a liability account. The asset Office Furniture was chosen because it represents the total of all of the office furniture that is owned. Since the transaction will increase the asset Office Furniture, that account should be debited. Accounts Payable was chosen because the furniture was bought on account (for credit). Since Accounts Payable is a liability and it has increased, it should be credited. Therefore, the correct answer is (C).

49. This question tests your knowledge of employment skills. It is always appropriate for an applicant to discuss matters that pertain directly to the conditions and terms of employment. Applicants should never discuss what they did not like about previous jobs or employers. Therefore, (D) is the correct answer.

50. This question tests your understanding of accounting concepts. Merchandise inventory is classified as an asset account. Sales Discount and Sales Returns and Allowances are both contra-income accounts that have the effect of reducing income. Purchase Returns and Allowances is a contra-purchases account and is not an income account at all. Interest Earned would be correctly classified as an Other Income account. (E) is correct.

51. This question asks you to refer to your knowledge of federal vocational education legislation. The Carl D. Perkins Act, reauthorized in 1998, allocates federal money for the training and development, in secondary and post-secondary institutions, of vocational skills. (A), (B), (C), and (D) are incorrect answers. (E) is the correct answer.

52. This question asks for the definition of an economic term. (A) is the correct definition. (B) is incorrect. It includes a value for resources used in production and does not take into account a value for services. (C) and (D) indicate a subtraction, and therefore a net answer rather than a gross, and are also incorrect. (E) accounts only for government expenditures and is incorrect.

53. This question asks you to recall your knowledge of computer terminology. A macro, by definition, is a sequence of stored keystrokes for frequently used functions within a software program, accessed with only one or two keystrokes. (A) and (C) refer to types of software and are incorrect. (D) refers to format capabilities in a word processing program, and is incorrect. (B) states that multiple functions are viewed on the screen simultaneously, and is incorrect. (E) is the correct answer.

54. This question asks you to apply your knowledge of formatting documents. (A) shows all parts of the business letter are keyed at the left margin, in correct full-block format. This is the correct answer. (B) and (D) show parts of the letter beginning at the center of a line and therefore are incorrect. (C) shows indented paragraphs, which is also incorrect. (E) is incorrect because it is missing the salutation, the signature line, and the typist's initials.

55. This question tests your knowledge of the use of computer equipment. Hard disks are clearly the choice if greater storage, faster access to data, longer useful life, or less maintenance is important. If low cost per disk is needed, then floppy disks are clearly an advantage over hard disks. The correct answer is (D).

56. This question tests your understanding of economic theory. Decreasing oil prices would allow more disposable income to be available, thus stimulating economic growth. It would also reduce inflation, because the reduction of oil prices would also reduce the cost of all products that use oil. Those reduced costs would be able to be passed along to the consumer in the form of lower prices, therefore lowering inflation. (A) is the correct answer.

57. This question asks you to apply your knowledge of business administration and management with regard to various careers available in this area. (A), (B), (D), and (E) all pertain to a career handling money and could be functions of a financial manager. (C) refers to a marketing career involving the production of goods and would not be a function of a financial manager. Therefore, (C) is the correct answer.

58. This question tests your understanding of curriculum goals. Computer literacy, records management, mail management, and time management are all skills that can be taught and improved by a business. Communication skills are the one competency that employees must possess as they enter the job. The correct answer is (B).

59. This question asks you to apply your knowledge of cooperative work programs. Cooperative work programs offer students classroom training and on-the-job work experience as part of their school program. (B) and (C) are secondary outcomes of cooperative office education and not primary goals. (D) and (E) are neither outcomes nor goals of cooperative office education programs. (A) is the correct answer.

60. This question tests your understanding of types of authority in business transactions. Vance gave Julia neither express (A) nor implied (B) authority to buy designer jeans. Nevertheless, the manufacturer, Casual Wear, had every reason to expect that Julia had authority regarding purchasing decisions because of her position as store manager. This is *apparent* authority. The correct answer, therefore, is (C). *Respondeat superior*, (E), does not apply because Julia did not cause harm to the manufacturer; she merely ran up a bill. An undisclosed principal, (D), is someone who uses somebody else as an agent for negotiations with a third party, often in situations where the agent pretends to be acting for himself or herself. Julia clearly is not doing this.

61. This question asks you to apply your knowledge of teaching pedagogy with respect to competency-based instruction. This method of teaching is prevalent in business education, specifically in skill-building areas of instruction. Competency-based programs are based on student achievement of specific objectives outlined in a course of study. These objectives direct the method and scope of instruction. (A) is the correct answer to this question. How students are evaluated, (B), and whether or not mastery has been achieved for job placement purposes, (C), are not underlying premises. (D) is also incorrect because objectives **need** to be shared in all types of instruction. (E) is also incorrect because objectives are specific for competency-based instruction. There should be no room for student interpretation.

62. This question tests your knowledge of marketing sales techniques. Odd pricing is a psychological pricing strategy that sets prices at odd amounts such as 19 cents, 49 cents, $19.95, and so on. Thus, pricing a shirt at $24.95 is an example of odd pricing, and (B) is correct.

63. This question tests your knowledge of word processing functions. Finding spelling errors and synonyms is not associated with the search function, but rather with the spell checking or thesaurus tools. Locating a file on the data disk or finding the source of a document on a data disk is not accomplished by a word processor's search function. Those items can be located using the Windows file management tool. A word processor can be used only to search for a character or set of characters in a text. (C) is the correct answer.

64. This question asks you to apply your knowledge of the philosophy of vocational education. (A), (C), (D), and (E) are all viable goals for a vocational business education program. The term "vocational," however, should trigger the idea of competencies and skill building. Vocational education programs use advisory councils and local employers of students to obtain constant feedback regarding employment needs of the local community. With regard to vocational education, this is the major focus and intention of a successful program. Therefore, (B) is the correct answer.

65. This question asks you to identify information related to business and consumer law. Qualified endorsements must add the words "Without recourse" to the regular endorsement in order to limit liability. Restrictive endorsements use "For deposit only" to limit the negotiability of the check to a specific activity. Full endorsements change the payee of the check by requiring the words "Pay to the order of" and the name of a new payee to be placed on the back of the check. Licensed endorsements do not exist. (D) is the correct choice.

66. This question asks you to apply your knowledge of cooperative education work programs. Cooperative education exists when a student receives formal training in the classroom and at a job site on a part-time basis. The document described in the question stem is the definition of a **training plan**. This is a required, signed statement by the student, teacher, and employer as to student responsibilities on the job. Therefore, (A) is the correct answer. (B), (C), (D), and (E) all refer to job-site activities, classroom activities included.

67. This question tests your understanding of basic accounting concepts. The basic accounting equation is: Total Assets minus Total Liabilities equals Net Worth. Therefore, (B) is the correct answer.

68. This question tests your knowledge of inventory evaluation methods in accounting. The FIFO method of inventory valuation assumes for cost purposes that inventory acquired first is sold first. During a time of rising prices, the merchandise purchased at

lower costs would be assumed to be sold first. Since that would leave a higher ending inventory figure, the cost of merchandise sold would be lower than that of a LIFO valuation system. The correct answer, therefore, is (E).

69. This question tests your knowledge of types of evaluative instruments. Objective tests are designed to measure only knowledge gained. This type of testing instrument does not allow the student to engage in any other form of test strategy. The correct answer, therefore, is (E)

70. This question asks you to use your knowledge of the objectives of business education. Students completing a business education curriculum should have a higher level of skills than simply identification or awareness of skills and trends. Knowledge of investment concepts is also not the overall objective of a business education curriculum. Students should be able to attain and utilize business skills and knowledge in order to be successful. Therefore, (C) is correct.

71. This question asks you to apply your knowledge of insurance under the topic of business law. (A), (C), and (E) are types of insurance, not legal documents, and are therefore incorrect. (D) refers to an event that may result in loss or gain and is therefore uninsurable; this is also an incorrect answer. The definition of insurable interest is a financial interest that a person has in the life of another or in property. Therefore, (B) is the correct answer. This is a legal requirement to purchase insurance.

72. This question asks you to apply your knowledge of tracking pedagogy with regards to special needs students. Special needs students require constant repetition of drills and review of what has been taught. Therefore, (D) is the correct answer. Lecturing (rather than hands-on instruction), competition, use of abstract examples, and the anxiety of frequent tests are all techniques that would increase the frustration level of a special needs student.

73. This question tests your knowledge of taxation. Federal and state income taxes are paid by the employee only. Workers compensation premiums are paid by the employer. The only tax paid equally by the employer and employee is FICA. The correct answer is (D).

74. This question tests your knowledge of teaching strategies. The question indicates the unit, and therefore the skills taught, should be at a higher level. Identification, use, and categorizing are clearly introductory skills. Balancing statements is not a higher level learning activity. Analysis and interpretation are higher level learning skills that should be addressed in an advanced unit. Therefore, (E) is the correct answer.

75. This question asks you to apply your knowledge of accounting concepts. A flow statement of incomes and expenses is an income statement. A balance sheet is a statement of condition that shows assets and the claims against the assets (liabilities and owner's equity). The correct answer is (C).

76. This question asks you to apply your knowledge of word processing and desktop publishing terminology, specifically document preparation. (A), (B), (C), and (D), all refer to placing items in some type of order, whether it be numerical, alphabetical, or categorical. These are incorrect answers. (E) refers to the placement of text information on a page in a manner that allows for ease of use and readability by the reader. (E) is therefore the correct answer.

77. This question asks you to evaluate your knowledge of oral communications. When a speaker is making any type of speech or presentation, the speaker's main goal is to persuade the audience to do something. Analysis or criticism may occur in a speech or presentation. However, excellent speakers know how to persuade their audience into action. The correct answer is (D).

78. This question tests your ability to calculate inventory turnover. The merchandise inventory turnover tells a retailer how many times the inventory is theoretically sold in its entirety during a fiscal period. To calculate the merchandise inventory, you must divide the cost of goods sold by the average inventory. The correct answer is (C).

79. This question asks you to apply your knowledge of finance. Book value and par value, (A) and (B), refer to an assigned dollar value that is printed on a stock certificate and are both incorrect answers. (D) is also incorrect. A stock could be liquidated at a far lower price than its market value. The terms in (E) both refer to the same value—issuing

price is par value—so (E) is incorrect. Market value of common stock reflects the price investors are willing to pay for a share of stock. This may also be called current trading price. Therefore, (C) is the correct answer.

80. This question tests your understanding of the various forms of business organization. Partnerships and sole proprietorships cease to exist when the current owner or owners no longer are a part of the business. Only a corporation is able to continue to exist as new owners come and go. (A) is the correct response.

81. This question asks you to apply your knowledge of the U.S. Postal System, a topic taught in the Office Procedures curriculum. (A) and (B) are both considered first-class mail and require first-class postage. They are incorrect answers. A postal zone does not determine the category of mailing and therefore makes (C) an incorrect choice. (D) refers to volume mailings or bulk mailings that are subject to a reduced rate. (D) is also incorrect. (E) is the correct answer. Newspapers and periodicals are mailed second-class by the U.S. Postal Service.

82. This question tests your understanding of entering and verifying data. (B), (C), (D), and (E) are letter codes for a Video Display Terminal, Cathode Ray Tube, Continuous Phase Modulation, and a Central Processing Unit, respectively. UPC stands for Universal Price Coding, which is a bar code system for pricing and inventory control. (A) is the correct answer.

83. This question asks you to apply your knowledge of data processing (computer) terminology. (B), (C), and (D) are not electronic methods of data storage and are incorrect answers. (A) is electronic but does not allow for random retrieval of data, only sequential. Therefore, (E) is the correct answer. Hard and floppy disks are magnetic options for data storage and allow for random retrieval of information.

84. This question tests your knowledge of the various types of mail. Special-delivery mail, first-class mail, and airmail all provide no proof that the document was delivered. Insured mail has proof of insurance that is provided to the sender. Only certified mail requires the receiver of the document to sign for it when it is delivered. The correct answer is (A).

85. This question tests your knowledge of international trade and economics. When a nation imports more than it exports, there is always an increase in the outflow of its currency because the nation is spending more than it is receiving. The correct answer is (C).

86. This question tests your knowledge of curriculum development. A business curriculum must focus on larger issues than ever before. No longer do business educators teach skills that focus only on specific jobs, since the job market changes so frequently. The correct answer is (A).

87. This question tests your knowledge of business mathematics. The terms 2/10, n/30 means that a 2 % discount will be given if the payment is made within 10 days of the invoice date. After 10 days the entire bill is due, with no discount for prompt payment. In this case, the purchase was made on June 1 and the payment made on June 9. Since that is less than 10 days, the discount applies. To calculate the discount, multiply $3,000 x 0.02. The resulting answer should be $60. The correct answer is (B).

88. This question asks you to apply your knowledge of topics covered in an office procedures curriculum. (A), (B), (C), and (E), are all typical responsibilities of a receptionist and are covered in the curriculum. (D) refers to a managerial task and would not be performed typically by a person hired as a receptionist. Therefore, (D) is the correct answer.

89. This question tests your knowledge of the fiscal and monetary policy of the Federal Reserve System. The Federal Reserve System is in charge of establishing monetary policy as it relates to the supply of money and the printing and distribution of paper currency. The Fed also establishes the guidelines that must be followed by member banks. The Federal Reserve does not, however, deal with the various tax laws and their implementation. The correct answer, therefore, is (B).

90. This question asks you to apply your knowledge of business mathematics. Profit is calculated by subtracting cost of goods from sales. Choose an answer from (A) through (E) and multiply it by $1,200 (the selling price of each unit). From this answer, subtract $10,000 (fixed costs) and $200 (per unit) for variable costs. By process of elimination, (B) is the correct choice. 20 units x $1,200 price per unit = $24,000 total sales. Then, $24,000 total sales - $10,000 fixed costs - $4,000 variable costs = $10,000 profit. Therefore, the correct answer is (B).

91. This question asks you to apply your knowledge of office procedures. (A) through (D) are all acceptable examples of proper telephone etiquette for an office worker. (E) is not an acceptable example because the office worker is now attempting to complete two individual tasks simultaneously and may seem nonfocused (and possibly disrespectful) to the person on the telephone. (E), therefore, is the correct answer.

92. This question asks you to apply your knowledge of marketing concepts. There are four basic marketing decisions, collectively known as the four P's: product, price, promotion (communicating to buyers), and place (distributing the product). Together they comprise a product's marketing mix. (D) is not a consideration in the mix and is therefore the correct answer.

93. This question asks you to apply your knowledge of teaching pedagogy with relation to an introductory skill-building business course. (A), (B), (C), and (D) refer to either the cognitive or affective domains of learning. Objectives written in the affective domain are concerned with how students feel. Objectives written in the cognitive domain are concerned with what knowledge the student has obtained. (A), (B), (C), and (D) are incorrect answers. Objectives written in the psychomotor domain are concerned with skill building and how a student performs. (E) is therefore the correct answer.

94. This question asks you to apply your knowledge of business ethics. (A) through (D) are all strategies a business should follow to be ethical and ensure customer loyalty. (E), however, states that adequate customer service policies are acceptable. This is incorrect. Extensive customer-service policies are essential for a business to maintain a high ethical standard. (E) is therefore the correct answer.

95. This question tests your knowledge of basic accounting information. Beginning inventory (A) is used in the preparation of an income statement. (B) is also an amount calculated on the income statement. A checking account balance, (D), is computed in the check register, and a requisition, (E), is used as a source in the preparation of purchase orders. (C) is the correct answer.

96. This question tests your knowledge of word processing. Basic word processing software allows the user to change spelling, search and replace, move paragraphs, and number the pages automatically. Although many word processing programs can identify some grammatical errors, they cannot typically locate complex grammatical errors and word-choice errors. The correct answer, therefore, is (C).

97. This question tests your knowledge of negotiable instruments. Under Article 3, Part 1, Section 104 of the Uniform Commercial Code, a negotiable instrument is defined as "an unconditional promise or order to pay a fixed amount of money, with or without interest, ...payable on demand or at a definite time." Therefore, (C) is the correct answer.

98. This question asks you to apply your knowledge of professional business education through the eyes of a department chairperson or purchasing agent. Equipment purchased for use in a business education classroom must satisfy (A), (B), (C), and (E). These are all important factors in choosing equipment and are therefore incorrect answers. The least important factor listed is the instructor's familiarity with the equipment purchased. Constant updating of equipment is necessary to conform to current business trends in technology. Therefore, constant training of teachers to utilize new equipment also becomes necessary. (D) is not an important factor in choosing equipment and is therefore the correct answer.

99. This question tests your knowledge of the laws related to shipping of merchandise. F.O.B. Destination requires the title to be transferred when the seller delivers the goods to the destination. F.O.B. Shipping Point passes the title to the retailer at the time the goods are delivered to the carrier. The correct answer is (A).

100. This question asks you to apply your knowledge of office procedures. All of the choices listed are electronic methods of communicating information either by telephone or computer except (C). Express mail is a service the U.S. Postal System offers for delivering a package or envelope. (C), therefore, is the correct answer.

Chapter 7
Are You Ready? Last-Minute Tips

▶ ▶ ▶ ▶ ▶ ▶ ▶ ▶ ▶ ▶ ▶ ▶

Checklist

Complete this checklist to determine if you're ready to take your test.

❑ Do you know the testing requirements for teaching business education in the state(s) where you plan to teach?

❑ Have you followed all of the test registration procedures?

❑ Do you know the topics that will be covered in the *Business Education* test?

❑ Have you reviewed any textbooks, class notes, and course readings that relate to the business education topics in chapter 3?

❑ Do you know how long the test will take and the number of questions it contains? Have you considered how you will pace your work?

❑ Are you familiar with the test directions and the types of questions for your test?

❑ Are you familiar with the recommended test-taking strategies and tips?

❑ Have you practiced by working through the practice test questions at a pace similar to that of an actual test?

❑ If you are repeating a Praxis Series™ Assessment, have you analyzed your previous score report to determine areas where additional study and test preparation could be useful?

The day of the test

You should have ended your review a day or two before the actual test date. And many clichés you may have heard about the day of the test are true. You should

- Be well rested

- Take photo identification with you

- Take a supply of well-sharpened #2 pencils (at least three)

- Eat before you take the test, and take some food or a snack to keep your energy level up

- Be prepared to stand in line to check in or to wait while other test takers are being checked in

You can't control the testing situation, but you can control yourself. Stay calm. The supervisors are well trained and make every effort to provide uniform testing conditions, but don't let it bother you if the test doesn't start exactly on time. You will have the necessary amount of time once it does start.

You can think of preparing for this test as training for an athletic event. Once you've trained, and prepared, and rested, give it everything you've got. Good luck.

Appendix A
Study Plan Sheet

▶ ▶ ▶ ▶ ▶ ▶ ▶ ▶ ▶ ▶ ▶ ▶

Study Plan Sheet

See chapter 1 for suggestions on using this Study Plan Sheet.

STUDY PLAN						
Content covered on test	How well do I know the content?	What material do I have for studying this content?	What material do I need for studying this content?	Where can I find the materials I need?	Dates planned for study of content	Date completed

Appendix B
For More Information

▶ ▶ ▶ ▶ ▶ ▶ ▶ ▶ ▶ ▶ ▶ ▶

Appendix B: For More Information

Educational Testing Service offers additional information to assist you in preparing for the Praxis Series™ Assessments. *Tests at a Glance* booklets and the *Registration Bulletin* are both available on our Web site at **www.ets.org/praxis.**

General Inquires

Phone: 800-772-9476 or 609-771-7395 (Monday-Friday, 7:45 A.M. to 8:00 P.M., EST)
Fax: 609-771-7906

Extended Time

If you have a learning disability or if English is not your primary language, you can apply to be given more time to take your test. The *Registration Bulletin* tells you how you can qualify for extended time.

Disability Services

Phone: 866-387-8602 or 609-771-7780
Fax: 609-771-7165
TTY (for deaf or hard-of-hearing callers): 609-771-7714

Mailing Address

ETS–The Praxis Series
P.O. Box 6051
Princeton, NJ 08541-6051

Overnight Delivery Address

ETS–The Praxis Series
Distribution and Receiving Center
225 Phillips Blvd.
Ewing, NJ 08628-7435

NOTES

Maturity = $I = P \times R \times T$ + Amt borrowed
$$\boxed{M = P + I}$$

NOTES

141 6.67 .33
118.06

Ordinary $I = \dfrac{*}{360}$ (12 mth @ 30 days)
$$I = P \times R \times T$$

Exact 365 days
$$I = P \times R \times T$$

$$P = I / R \times T$$
$$R = I / P \times T$$